# FICTION WRITER'S HANDBOOK

Hallie &

# FICTION HAND

Harper & Row, Publishers

Whit Burnett

# WRITER'S
# BOOK

New York, Evanston, San Francisco, London

*1817*

FICTION WRITER'S HANDBOOK.
Copyright © 1975 by Hallie Burnett.
All rights reserved.
Printed in the United States of America.
No part of this book may be used or reproduced
in any manner whatsoever without written permission
except in the case of brief quotations
embodied in critical articles and reviews.
For information address Harper & Row, Publishers, Inc.,
10 East 53rd Street, New York, N.Y. 10022.
Published simultaneously in Canada
by Fitzhenry & Whiteside Limited, Toronto.

FIRST EDITION

*Designed by Dorothy Schmiderer*

---

Library of Congress Cataloging in Publication Data

Burnett, Hallie Southgate, date
  Fiction writer's handbook.

  Includes index.
  1. Fiction—Authorship.   I. Burnett, Whit, date
joint author.   II. Title.
PN3355.B78   1975        808'.025       74–1797
ISBN 0–06–010574–7

---

  76 77 78 79 10 9 8 7 6 5 4 3

Grateful acknowledgment is made for permission to reprint the following:

Excerpt from "Eine Kleine Nacht" by Peter de Vries reprinted from *STORY* Magazine, copyright 1935 by Story Magazine, Inc.

Excerpt from "A Dream of Angelo Zara" by Guido D'Agostino reprinted from *STORY* Magazine, copyright 1942 by Story Magazine, Inc.

Excerpt from "Noon Wine" from *Pale Horse, Pale Rider* by Katherine Anne Porter reprinted by permission of Harcourt Brace Jovanovich, Inc. Copyright 1936, 1964 by Katherine Anne Porter.

Excerpt from *Good Morning, Midnight* by Jean Rhys reprinted by permission of Harper & Row, Publishers, Inc. 1970.

Excerpt from "Warm River" from *The Complete Stories of Erskine Caldwell* by Erskine Caldwell, published by Little Brown and Company. Copyright 1932 by Richard Johns. Copyright renewed by Erskine Caldwell. By permission of the author.

Excerpt from "A Rose for Emily" from *Collected Stories of William Faulkner* by William Faulkner. Copyright 1930 by William Faulkner. Copyright renewed 1958 by William Faulkner. Reprinted by permission of Random House, Inc.

Excerpt from "My Side of the Matter" from *A Tree of Night and Other Stories* by Truman Capote. Copyright 1945 by Truman Capote. Reprinted by permission of Random House, Inc.

Excerpt from *The Notebooks of Henry James* by F. O. Mattheissen and Kenneth Murdock reprinted by permission of Oxford University Press, Inc. Copyright 1947 by Oxford University Press, Inc. Copyright renewed 1975 by Kenneth B. Murdock and Mrs. Peters Putnam.

Excerpt from "A Summer's Reading" from *The Magic Barrel* by Bernard Malamud reprinted by permission of Farrar, Straus, & Giroux, Inc. © 1956, 1958 by Bernard Malamud. This story originally appeared in *The New Yorker*.

Excerpt from *The Short Happy Life of Francis Macomber* by Ernest Hemingway. Copyright 1936 by Ernest Hemingway. Copyright renewed 1964 by Mary Hemingway. Reprinted by permission of Charles Scribner's Sons.

Excerpt from *Herzog* by Saul Bellow. Copyright © 1961, 1963, 1964 by Saul Bellow. Reprinted by permission of The Viking Press, Inc.

Excerpt from "Horsie" from *The Portable Dorothy Parker*. Copyright 1932, copyright renewed 1960 by Dorothy Parker. Reprinted by permission of The Viking Press, Inc.

Excerpt from *Winesburg, Ohio* by Sherwood Anderson. Copyright 1919 by B. W. Huebsch, Inc. Copyright renewed 1947 by Eleanor Copenhaver Anderson. Reprinted by permission of The Viking Press, Inc.

Excerpt from "Sherrel" by Whit Burnett from *STORY* Magazine, copyright 1931 by Whit Burnett and Martha Foley.

Excerpt from "Theodore and the Blue Danube" by Ludwig Bemelmans from *STORY* Magazine, copyright 1936 by Story Magazine, Inc.

Excerpt from "Address Unknown" by Kressmann Taylor from *STORY* Magazine, copyright 1938 by Story Magazine, Inc.

Excerpt from "The Man" by Mel Dinelli from *STORY* Magazine, copyright 1945 by Story Magazine, Inc.

Excerpt from "The Sunken Boat" by Robert Payne from *STORY* Magazine, copyright 1947 by Story Magazine, Inc.

Excerpt from "The Ubiquitous Wife" by Marcel Aymé and Whit Burnett from *STORY* Magazine, copyright © 1960 by Story Magazine, Inc.

Excerpt from "The Strange Notion" by Harold Helfer from *STORY* Magazine, copyright 1951 by Whit Burnett and Hallie Burnett.

Excerpt from "The Organizer" by Michael Thelwell from *Story: The Yearbook of Discovery/1968*, edited by Whit and Hallie Burnett, © 1968 by Scholastic Magazines, Inc.

Excerpt from "The Short Story from a Purely Personal View" by Hallie Burnett which originally appeared in the 1961 *Writer's Yearbook*. Copyright 1961 by F & W Publishing Corp.

Excerpt from *The Crack-Up* by F. Scott Fitzgerald. Copyright 1937 by Pocket Book Publishing Co., 1945 by New Directions Publishing Corporation. Copyright © 1964 by Frances Scott Fitzgerald Lanahan. Reprinted by permission of New Directions Publishing Corporation.

This book is dedicated to those particular individuals whose friendship, loyalty, and support made bearable the thirty years of our combined companionship—Whit's, mine, and *STORY's*—in the difficult times of keeping a quality magazine alive and well; and memorably, wonderfully rewarding in the good times of publishing authors we admired. There are also some newer friends who have helped make this book possible:

Norman Mailer
Guido D'Agostino
Mary O'Hara
Turnley Walker
William Saroyan
Erskine Caldwell
Truman Capote
J. D. Salinger
Jesse Stuart
Eddie Cohen
Ken McCormick
Riley Hughes
Frances Steloff
William Shirer
Matthew Huttner
Allan Seager
Whitney Anne Beekman Burnett

Eleanor Gilchrist
Cass Canfield
Emanie and Toby Philips
Happy and Richard Wathen
William Peden
Julie and Walter Langsam
Alexander Clark
Morley Callaghan
M. R. Robinson
Louise Bates
Harry Hansen
Anita Berke
Joseph Vergara
Rhoda Dreifus
John Southgate Burnett
Ralph D. Gardner

Other friends whose loyalty and friendship are not forgotten:

Bernadine and Harry Scherman
John Gunther
Elizabeth Southgate

Carson McCullers
Gorham Munson
John Reddy

# CONTENTS

Flaubert never published a treatise on his literary principles; indeed, it was one of his principles not to do so, but to embody them in the one place where he thought they belonged—his fiction.

*Maupassant and Flaubert*
—FRANCIS STEEGMULLER

I firmly believe every book was meant to be written.
—MARCHETTE CHUTE

# FOREWORD

FOR SOME YEARS before his death on Easter Day, 1973, Whit and I had planned to write together a book on the short story. We never quite got around to it, for various reasons: among these, our attempts for almost three decades to keep the magazine *STORY* alive; the books we wrote or edited separately or together on other subjects; our teaching, lecturing, and editing for other publishing houses.

Now, with the encouragement of Whit's old friend Cass Canfield, who at one time was the publisher of STORY Press books, and Joseph Vergara, a sympathetic and knowledgeable editor, I have written a book which I hope and believe will express Whit's own very personal feelings, were he alive, on the art and craft of fiction writing—the short story and the novel. For those thirty years we worked together, edited together and, while we did not write together, we edited each other's work and shared most of our professional and private lives and interests. It would be impossible to write such a book as this without that cooperation and understanding.

Whit left some notes, embellished with his own special brand of humor. Many of these were from lectures he had given through the years. He could be a very funny, impromptu speaker, but since his humor was not of the kind to be plotted out carefully in advance, these notes have been of benefit more by what they evoked than by their details. There were also some pages on writing the short story, and many of these have been incorporated in this book.

Beyond this, one must speak of Whit's lifetime of championing the rights of an author to say what he wanted in the way he wanted to say it; his patience and belief in the discipline and care of talent, without which, he insisted, no good writing is ever achieved; and his unflagging delight in each new talent as it was discovered, by himself or by anyone else. Someone said he was "the professional's professional." Nothing would have pleased him more than that.

H. B.

# PREFACE

## by Norman Mailer

I DON'T KNOW if it still is true, but in the years I went to Harvard (so long ago as 1939 to 1943) they used to give a good writing course. In fact, it was not one good course, but six. English A was compulsory for any Freshman who did not get a very good mark on the English College Entrance Boards, and five electives followed, English A–1, English A–2, up to English A–5, a vertiginous meeting place for a few select talents whose guide was no less than Professor Robert Hillyer, the Pulitzer Prize poet. By Senior year, I was taking English A–5, in fact I must have been one of the few students in Harvard history who took all but one of the writing courses (A–4 I missed) and must even be one of the few living testimonials to the efficacy of half a dozen classes in composition and the art of the short story. I entered college as a raw if somewhat generous-hearted adolescent from Brooklyn who did not know the first thing about a good English sentence (that is, its God-given ability to show tensile strength—don't take out a word!) and left four years later as a half-affected and much imperfect Harvard man who had nonetheless had the great good fortune to find the passion of his life before he was twenty. I wanted to be a writer. And had the further good luck to conceive this passion in Freshman year in a *compulsory* course in elementary composition. That much will be granted to the forces of oppression.

English A at Harvard in 1939 put its emphasis on teaching a student to write tolerably well—an ability we could certainly use over the next three years. The first stricture of the course was a wise one: writing is an extension of speech we were told. So we were instructed to try to write with something of the ease with which we might speak, and that is a good rule for beginners. In time it can be absorbed, taken for granted, and finally disobeyed. The best writing comes obviously out of a precision we do not and dare not employ when we speak, yet such writing still has the ring of speech. It is a style in short that can take you a life to achieve.

At Harvard, however, they knew how to get us to begin, and there were fine men teaching English A: among others Theodore Morrison, Mark Schorer and Albert Guérard, if my memory does not trick me, and men like Robert Gorham Davis and Murray Kempton were there to take us up the ladder of the electives from A–1 to A–5. Over four years of such courses one would have had to have a determined purchase on lack of talent not to improve. I improved. In those four years, I learned a little about sentence construction and more about narrative pace; en route I was able to pick up some of the literary ego a young writer needs to keep going through the contradictory reactions of others to his work. If there is one reason above others for taking a writing course, it is to go through the agonizing but indispensable recognition that one's own short story, so clear, so beautiful, so powerful, and so *true*, so definite in its meaning or so well balanced in its ambiguity, has become a hundred different things for other writers in your class. Even the teacher does not get your buried symbols, or worse, does not like them. Being a young writer in a writing course can bruise the psyche as much as being a novice in the Golden Gloves can hurt your head. There is punishment in recognizing how much more punishment will yet have to be taken. Yet the writing course has its unique and ineradicable value. For you get to see the faces of those who like and do not quite like your work, you hear their voices, and so you can gain some comprehension of the perversities of an audience's taste (as when, for example, they like a story by a writer that you despise). You can even come to recognize how a fine piece of prose can draw the attention of an audience together. If it happens to you, if you write a piece and everyone in the room listens as if there is nourishment for one ear—their own—then it will not matter afterward if you hear a dozen separate reactions, for you will have at last the certainty that you are a writer. Your work has effect—in some small way you have begun to enter the life and intelligence of others. Then you are not likely to stay away from writing; indeed, if you get even a glimpse of such a reaction from one of your paragraphs, you will discover that you must have more such paragraphs. You will want more of the ineffable pleasure of such attention.

This much said for the value of a writing course—that you learn a little of the impact of your work on strangers—it may seem curious why I proceed then to offer a preface for a book which could appear to claim the opposite: that by being held in your hands and reasonably perused, it will aid you to become a writer. I would reply that in great part it can; it can serve as a crucial enrichment to students afloat in writing courses not nearly so good as the ones I had the fortune to take at Harvard, and it can certainly serve as an indispensable primer to lead any beginning writer through the early maze of that mystery which surrounds the near-to-sacred and most terrifying empty spaces of the empty page. I do not pretend to be an authority on books which teach how to write fiction, but I know I have not read a better one for beginning writers. And to anyone who is removed by temperament or by geography from the opportunity to take a writing course, this book presents a way to begin, and it is a good way, and it is an agreeably written book considering that little is more difficult to write about agreeably than matters of literary instruction.

So I can offer this preface in confidence. *Fiction Writer's Handbook* is wise and comprehensive and surprisingly full of touches of lore. It has hints for one's craft. A beginner at writing can sleep with this book. There is enthusiasm in the pages. Its author, after all, has lived with the idea of writing for the larger part of her life, and that is probably a disappearing culture. Not many can be left in that small world of a few writers and teachers and editors who believed there were not many vocations more honored than writing, nor many occupations more interesting than to encourage the talent of a young writer. Today a young man or woman of talent goes to college with the idea of getting into film, or TV, or media, or rock or even group encounter. They may even have a thing about writing. Like it's interesting. Like they may want to get into that, too. Words can be laid down for serial communicative connections.

Of course, says the avuncular voice, it was different in my day. We were taught to jeer at phrases like "serial communicative connections." If McLuhan had appeared, we might have burned him. As a generation, we were still in the shadow of Fitzgerald and Faulkner and Hemingway, and almost in the life of Wolfe and Dos Passos and Steinbeck and Farrell. We had only one idea. It was to write. It was to become an American writer. That was what we all wanted. It was our religion and our revolution, our love affair and our sport, our dedication and our vice. We did not have any other ideals. And only a very small code. It was to be determined in our cynicism. You could not be a good writer unless you were profoundly cynical.

Needless to say, a lot of us had the luck to meet and be helped by that small group of editors and writers and teachers who also thought it was important to be a writer, and we were helped on our way. One of that group was a very modest man who had a beautiful white goatee by the time I met him. I was still eighteen and wholly embarrassed by my inability to speak a single interesting word to him, and he was shy and embarrassed by his inability to draw me out. We had lunch together and searched for topics to talk about. Once he asked me if I knew anything about chamber quartets. It was obvious at the instant that he played in such a group, and I, full of the roller hockey and touch football of Brooklyn streets—two sewers apart were our goal lines—blurted out in my new-found Harvard voice that miserably I was an ignoramus at such things. And we nodded painfully and enthusiastically at each other and kept eating in longer silences.

Yet it was one of the more luminous meals of my life. For the man with whom I was at lunch was a legend. And his magazine, *STORY*, was its own legend, and young writers in the late thirties and the years of the Second World War used to dream of appearing in its pages about the way a young rock group might feel transcendent in these hours with the promise of a spread in *Rolling Stone*. The man was taking me to lunch out of his magazine's small budget because I had won in the late spring of my Sophomore year, a short story contest for college writers. That was the first powerful and happy event of my career, and I do not know that there have been that many good ones since. It was as powerful a charge of happiness as I found in my adolescence. I suppose I felt as good as if I had just won the Olympics. So the lunch to commemorate this event could not have been bad no matter how little communication took place, and I was left with a feeling of the man's kindliness, his literary kindliness, and his wistful desire to offer his own fine hand into the elaboration of that rarest of a nation's stock—its quintessential literary culture.

In later years we would run into one another from time to time, and greet each other warmly. We were not friends because we did not begin to have the kind of opportunities which bring people together and make them friends. But we were certainly friendly acquaintances, we were invariably pleased to see each other. We had each, after all, been good for the other. Each of us had in some small way a confirmation of the other's idea of how things perhaps ought to go. So it is a pleasure to write this preface, and inform you that the author of this book, Hallie Burnett, lived that literary life with her husband, and their most specific literary culture is in this book. The man's name, of course, is Whit Burnett and I promise that the reader will hear more than a bit about him in chapters to come, and will have the literary experience of acquiring more than a little wisdom with relatively little work. That is the magic of literature— it is opposed to the laws of the gravity of effort—and some clues to the process of this levitation of language are in the pages which follow by Hallie Burnett.

# I

# SELF-EXAMINATION OF
# A FICTION WRITER

# 1
# WHY WRITE?

AN EXTRAORDINARY WRITERS' CONFERENCE was held one summer at Boulder, Colorado, under the poet (then Dean of College) Theodore Davison, who gathered together a faculty of writers which included Robert Frost, Tom Wolfe, Jean Stafford, and Whit Burnett (then young and bearded) among others. Some of the women students fainted from the altitude or went a little crazy, and the writing faculty lectured, read manuscripts, insulted students who couldn't write, and had a pretty good time.

One day Robert Frost came across Whit when he was reading a rare volume of Frost's poems—which Frost borrowed, but never returned. A few years later he did send Whit an easily available volume of his collected poems in place of the rare book, but without apology. Obviously Frost made no bones about pleasing himself first. When an intrepid student asked him one day why anyone should write in the first place, Frost's answer was unequivocal:

"I don't know why *you* should write, but I know why I do. I don't get the same satisfaction out of doing anything else."

To get more satisfaction out of writing than out of anything else certainly is part of what it means to be a writer. With distractions all around us, singleness of purpose is essential in getting at the natural rewards and pleasures of the tasks we set for ourselves. Any one of us may be asked one day, "Why write?" and it is well to be prepared with a satisfactory answer. It is well to be able to say we don't get the same pleasure from doing anything else.

But why does anyone want to *be* a writer?

To be a success, of course. To be read, to be loved, to be listened to—maybe to write only best sellers, those baskets into which most publishing houses prefer to put their eggs. But never mind. All authors are entitled to some illusions, and chances are if one manages a certain dedication and perseverance, if one applies the seat of the pants to the seat of the chair as Sinclair Lewis once advised, and ignores rejections, laughs at being (so far) unappreciated, and Keeps the Faith, Baby, why, he might just get somewhere in the end. *Somewhere.*

But man or woman, you've got to make up your mind. You can't be forever that uncertain beginner who goes around asking practically anyone, teacher or editor or wife, "But do *you* think I'm a writer? Is writing for me going to be worth the time and energy and sacrifices and maybe ridicule I'll have to spend on it? Should I keep on writing? Or should I give it all up and become a millionaire instead?"

There is that old story about J. P. Morgan, who was asked how much his yacht cost by a man who wondered if he could afford one: "If you've got to ask the cost, you can't afford it." If you need to be constantly reassured and encouraged, if you must lean on the opinions of others, you can't afford to write. You can't afford the time and effort "to bear the toil of writing," as E. M. Forster has said, so forget the whole thing if you can. It is better to know your limitations early and then turn to something else, either making millions, or another form of writing that won't demand such stoicism of you. Katherine Anne Porter has warned us that "to follow an art, you've got to give up something."

The need to write originates God-knows-where. But in any true writer the impulse has probably always been there, gathering strength in some such region as his solar plexus, tantalizing him to get on with his creation. Each time he reads something he wishes he had written, and covets the author's role, he is preparing his own self-image as a writer. Whenever he dwells overlong on deeds or behavior or injustices to someone loved, hated, or merely observed with an obsessive interest, he is already practicing his trade. When he arranges facts and fancies and words to express some obscure inner sense of form that is entirely his own imagining, and strives to create dramatic situations from bare and undramatic facts, he is surely on his way.

What does it matter if this introspection, these imaginary afterthoughts, do make neurotics out of anyone else? Or that such practices also fit thieves, liars, and actors? The incurable writer will happily admit he might have been all these (but not in his work!), and be grateful that nature has provided him with such built-in understanding of characters he may eventually use as his own. If the end of most men is right living, as has been said, the end of the writer is the strength and honesty of what he creates with the equipment he has and from observations he will make. He cannot afford to let anything in daily life go by without examining it after the fact; he will rarely fail to explore any nagging feeling of remorse, or guilt, or jealousy, or apprehension, or love, or smug self-satisfaction. But heaven help him if he indulges these traits once he has ceased being a writer—or if he never starts!

There is abundant evidence that those successful writers who keep at their labors for more than one brief season, devoting energy and hours of work not exceeded in any other profession, do so not only because of the satisfaction this gives them but also from the intensity of their desire to write. Katherine Anne Porter has said that she started out with nothing in the world but "a kind of passion, a driving desire." Eudora Welty has said of Willa Cather that she "embodied passion" in her work, and Somerset Maugham, in his still valuable book *The Summing Up,* asserted that "we do not write because we want to; we write because we must." Gentle French Abbé Dimnet once explained simply that "the experience of most artists is that the quality of their production is in keeping with the intensity of their wish."

*Why write?* Is it because one is a born raconteur, and has tales to tell? But it is possible to talk so well one never has time to write. The verbal storyteller needs a Chaucer or a Boccaccio on hand to record what he says.

*Why write?* Some believe a writer's life is exciting and full of compensations, financial rewards and fame. Yet we all know that the last years of F. Scott Fitzgerald were leadened by failure, and the biographies of most famous writers reveal distressing fluctuations between success and lost confidence, achievement and rejection. Virginia Woolf suffered intensely each time her work was brought before the public; Sherwood Anderson, who claimed that only through writing could he "get rid of self," was so depressed by rejection that from time to time he gave it all up to go back into the business world he hated, a kind of closet from which he emerged only when he could no longer stand the "dishonesty."

It was not until late in life that William Faulkner was awarded the Nobel Prize for Literature with its accompanying $40,000 prize money at a time when, it was rumored, all his books were out of print.

Some years earlier *STORY,* in one of its characteristic depressions, bought a story from Faulkner for $25—the price then paid to Lord Dunsany, Luigi Pirandello, Thomas Mann, Frank O'Connor, Ferenc Molnár, or any promising unknown who appeared in our magazine. And Faulkner was grateful. "I have become so damned frantic trying to make a living and keeping my grocer, etc. from putting me in bankruptcy for the last year that nothing I or anybody else ever wrote seems worth anything to me any more," he wrote.

*Why write?* Both Stendhal and Maugham claimed they wrote at the beginning of their careers to make an impression on women, although to Stendhal hope of fame was even more compelling. And *STORY*'s $500 prize money to Richard Wright in the 1930s took him off the Works Progress Administration and gave him the security he needed to go on to *Native Son* and *Black Boy* (STORY Press–Harper), thus launching a new force in Negro writing in America years before the racial expressions of today.

"Art," says Madariaga, "is a bridge of matter between spirit and spirit."

It was in the 1930s that a young man began sending in a story a day from the west coast, single-spaced on yellow second sheets, not all under the same name. When "The Daring Young Man on the Flying Trapeze" and several others were bought and published under the author's real name, William Saroyan, he wrote the editors of *STORY* a letter. He wanted to be a writer, because:

"I believe in what I am saying firmly. I believe the tremendous powers of the Word are only beginning to be recognized. In my writing I wish to use the Word in a way that will inevitably improve living . . . I wish to relate and interpret the story of man on earth as I understand his story . . . Through my writing I hope to go beneath and beyond surfaces; to see; to know; to declare; to make known; to rejoice!

"I plan to accomplish these (and other) ends through prose: short stories, novels, plays, prose poems and any other form of expression I find necessary to invent in order best to carry my thoughts and feelings. I plan to write in a way that will move the heart and the mind, in clear and simple prose."

*Why write?* How many reasons need a writer have? Well, there is that agreeable one of setting our own work hours and following the dictates of our own imaginations. And it is gratifying to be paid for pleasure one has had in private, when satisfaction in the thing itself is at least as great as the dollars and cents one's work may earn.

But then there *is* the money, which, with extraordinary success, may result from being on best-seller lists, from being sold to films, and from large paperback sales, all of which will, more than anything else, impress our friends and family.

*Why write?* We have freedom and the excuse to read and write without interruption; to be neurotic without censure; to experiment in love, or withdraw from society altogether if we are bored or demand solitude; and to travel and plunge into new experiences with the accepted excuse of gathering material and refertilizing our imagination. Writers are always permitted a few idiosyncrasies in their lives, once they have proved they are writers, and most of us know how to make the most of such privileges.

*Why write?* "Writing is a compulsive, and delectable thing," wrote Henry Miller. "Writing is its own reward."

*Why write?* The late J. Donald Adams of *The New York Times* wrote that writing itself is a form of catharsis, a purge of all the sins of omission or commission, insults, tragedies, and humors that have befallen individual man. Thus the writer, using the freedom of his imagination, has the benefit of being his own psychoanalyst, and where else outside of love or religion can the burdens of living and dying be so freely expressed and confessed?

Finally, the bonus we have above most arts is the availability of the greatest coaches and teachers, those timeless writers who have gone before us to challenge our small satisfactions, prod our waning ambitions, and inspire us to go deeper into the human condition as Dostoevski and Tolstoi and Mann and Flaubert and Austen and Joyce and Proust and all the rest did for us long ago. We won't achieve as much, but to refer to Robert Frost again, we as writers should still take our writing with all the seriousness we can muster —but never ourselves. Saroyan has said he started out writing to improve himself, and then kept on to improve everybody else.

*Why write?*
*What else?*

# 2
# EQUIPMENT OF A WRITER

THE WRITER'S NATURAL EQUIPMENT is probably no more complex than that of a singer or a painter, but the use of his talents is infinitely more varied. Thomas Wolfe speaks of the compulsion to write as an enormous black cloud bursting over his head, and other writers have described the onset of writing as a state of chaos out of which one must work compulsively to bring order.

What qualities must a writer have then, and develop, to bring a tale or novel through its logical development, to untangle the various threads of impressions and inconsistencies to give a viable meaning to the tag ends of character, event, and emotion gathered and waiting in one's conscious and subconscious mind?

Ben Jonson said that a writer first must judge rightly of himself before he can satisfactorily write of others; and to try to achieve anything "is in vain, without a natural wit and a poetical nature."

To try to assess one's natural qualifications is not the same thing, necessarily, as judging oneself with humility. One may know something about his own talent he has not yet succeeded in expressing either to his own satisfaction or to an editor's, and this careful evaluation is an essential means to a life of continuing creativity. It does not end here. A writer is constantly having to prove himself anyway, not only to an editor, and a public, but to himself. There is no point at which the writer may relax and say, "Well now, that is done"; at least not for long. What a writer has done may be forgotten. What he must do in the future must always surpass, in the writer's mind at least, anything he has done before.

Whit said an author's needs are simple. He needs four things: the ability to see; to remember; to reflect; to project. Anything else is a refinement of these qualities, and that is important too.

So let us make a kind of grocery list of qualities by which we may judge ourselves and other writers, the equipment that, with luck, will take our writing in the direction we want it to go. Let us cultivate:

1. Belief in the fiction voice: A fictional point of view
2. A footlight sense: The value of dramatic elements
3. Practice of honesty: Clear-sightedness
4. Empathy and compassion. Understanding
5. The fertilizing senses: Sight, hearing, smell, touch, and intuition
6. Imagination and a selective memory: Reflections, daydreaming
7. Love of language: Words, phrases, images
8. Style; wit; irony
9. Regularity and capacity for work: Pursuit of excellence
10. Talent; audacity. A touch of genius

## 1. Belief in the Fiction Voice: A Fictional Point of View

One may commence with talent and a burning desire to write, but the writer does not go far without an unqualified belief that only in fiction can the truths one knows be adequately expressed and developed. We must also have a belief in the physical and emotional reality of characters we have created, or evoked, and the inevitability of events we have made happen in their lives. We must be convinced that bare facts frequently lie, and only by imaginative probing and sometimes remembering, can we show life as it is, truth as it must be, and the unarguable reality of our vision.

The most essential task of any novelist, short story writer, dramatist, or poet—those realists who have no guide but their own imaginations; those imaginative artists who bring flights of fancy down to earth—must be to strengthen the quality of belief itself. Any faltering, any doubt the writer feels may defeat the credibility of what he has written, and characters he has presented will remain slick, wooden, and without sincerity. Hemingway has said that any reader knows when a writer fakes; and the writer himself must be the first to know the moment of his cheating.

Belief, among other things, is a matter of focus, is keeping one's eyes firmly on the ball. If a writer in the process of telling a tale turns from his game to the distraction of a plane flying overhead, he gives every indication that he has ceased to believe in the importance of his endeavor, and our own interest wanders. A supplicant who prays can only believe in God's presence if all other thoughts are put aside and his act of devotion is faithfully directed.

Everyone is familiar with characters in fiction or drama more real than persons we once knew well in life. Lear is unforgettable, more real than the friends with whom we had dinner the night we first saw the play. Huck Finn and Babbitt were read in school and remembered, even though the name of our teacher is lost. The creators of these characters never ceased believing in their fiction or questioned the truth of their characters' existences.

Richard Wright once wrote that although in *Native Son* he used characters he'd known in life, it was not possible for him to account completely for the results. "The more closely the author thinks of why he wrote, the more he comes to regard his imagination as a kind of self-generating cement which glued his facts together, and his emotions as a kind of dark and obscure designer of those facts. Reluctantly, he comes to the conclusion that to account for his book is to account for his life." But many generations now have felt that Bigger as a character stands alone because he was so clearly understood by his creator. And it was this understanding that gave Wright his stature and his *raison d'être* as an emotional novelist.

J. D. Salinger created characters so completely visual that one critic stated he had to distrust Salinger the man, because if his characters were *not* real, in the sense of having actual birth certificates and Social Security numbers, then what sort of liar was Salinger that he made us believe in them so profoundly?

And we all know how the printer of Katherine Mansfield's early novella *At the Bay* exclaimed when he could not resist reading what he was printing, "But these kids are *real!*" As idealized characters from Katherine Mansfield's own New Zealand childhood, they had expressed her homesickness and nostalgia in a way that only the best fiction can do.

The quality of belief, in character, in fate, in the senses; the images that crowd into one's mind larger and truer than life—this is what gives the writer both his freedom to create and his value in interpreting the world and human nature. A writer has his own life and unique experiences to write from, but unless his invented world becomes more real than any other, he will not take us far into the world of his imagination. And what we "invent by intuition," says Radhakrishnan, is easy enough to "prove by logic," if we retain our belief in the inner, imaginative world.

## 2. A Footlight Sense: The Value of Dramatic Elements

When Somerset Maugham said all good writers ought to develop a "footlight sense," he was giving away a particular secret of his trade. Maugham himself succeeded first as a dramatist, and however critical our judgment of his novels and short stories currently may be, no one has ever denied his professional skill or his understanding of an audience—his own "footlight sense," his readability and capacity to hold our attention. A writer must have an audience—readers who accept us, who are moved by what we have written, and who are compelled to read on with appreciation and compliance—an audience to stay until the end of the last act.

Drama is created from an author's awareness of human inconsistencies, incongruities, absurdities, and surprises translated into believable characters, scenes, and situations. Dramatist Harold Hayes said at Wagner College some years ago: "The essence of drama is that man cannot walk away from the consequences of his own deeds." And it is this essence that is distilled in our fiction as in our plays.

Many of the writers first printed over the years in STORY turned out to have a particular gift for the theater. Pirandello called short stories the "goose eggs of literature," and in our combined forty years of editing we have seen many of these goose eggs hatched in novels, while others have become swans on the Broadway stage.

A number of years ago we assembled a collection from STORY representing some of the more interesting talents brought to light in our magazine during the 1940s, a significant period in the development of the short story. It was then that J. D. Salinger, Truman Capote, Joseph Heller, Norman Mailer, and other new and previously unpublished writers appeared for the first time in our magazine —from Harvard, from New Orleans, and from the war zone, bringing freshness of vision and original treatment to both old and new subject matter.

The end results, the stories, were what we were after, however, and only incidentally were we interested in the authors' personalities or the other achievements that lay behind their works. We had too little time left over from reading manuscripts, for one thing. Also, as a young writer's first producer, in a sense, we were most concerned with the quality of his work as we presented it to our readers —more modestly to be sure than a play on Broadway, but on a level with other professional writers, and backed enthusiastically by the editors.

Yet it did not come as a complete surprise to learn, as we assembled the biographies, that a large percentage of those whose stories were included in *Fiction of the Forties* (in Britain, two volumes, *Fiction of a Generation*) had also, one way or another, found some recognition in the theater.

Some had already had this success. Erskine Caldwell, an old friend and contributor long before his play *Tobacco Road* was a great hit on Broadway, had been well known since his *God's Little Acre* was brought to trial by the New York Society for the Suppression of Vice. Whit had testified in Erskine's behalf and lent him an overcoat to wear on a cold day since he'd come up from the South in lightweight clothes. By the 1940s, Erskine had his own overcoat and his fame was secure.

There were other young authors, like J. William Archibald, a script writer for Hitchcock films, whose adaptation of Henry James's *Turn of the Screw* into *The Innocents* was then a critical and financial success both in New York and on the London stage; and Tennessee Williams, whose play *The Glass Menagerie* had recently been produced, some years after he'd written thanking *STORY* editors for the acceptance of his first short story, and informing the editors that he was at that time a theater usher and a dishwasher in a restaurant.

In this volume we printed a short story, "The Man" by Mel Dinelli, which was soon adapted as a play, with very few changes for the stage. Here perhaps is the simplest example of translating a short story into play form. It was a tale of suspense, and it succeeded as the thriller of that season.

Against a simple domestic background the story opens:

"Mrs. Gillis's roomer, Mr. Armstrong, tried to warn her that morning before he left on his business trip," that he thought it was reckless of her to have hired a strange young man to clean her house when she would be alone there with him all day.

Mrs. Gillis is amused; and when Howard, the young man, comes down the walk, Mr. Armstrong is relieved to see he looks frail and harmless. "So that's the critter who's been causing me all this mental anguish," he says, and everything is fine, except that Mrs. Gillis's old dog, Sarah, comes out from under the stove and growls. All this in the short story is transferred almost intact onto the stage.

Mr. Armstrong leaves and Mrs. Gillis takes Howard to a closet storeroom at the back of the house, where she gives him an apron. The existence of this storeroom is revealed at about the same moment both in story and play.

Oddly, Howard refuses the apron, because it has "spots on it."

" 'Spots?' Mrs. Gillis took the apron. 'Why, that's paint. No dirt in dried paint, son,' she said.

" 'If you don't mind, I'd rather not wear it.' "

During the rest of that day the situation develops with predictable intensity. When Howard accuses Mrs. Gillis of spying on him, she tries to reassure him that she was "interested in young men. I have two sons of my own—they're in the Service." She shows him their photographs.

"So that's why you hate me!" Howard says. "I see it all now!"

"Hate you? Why, whatever gave you—"

Poor Mrs. Gillis suggests he stop work. She offers to make him some tea. She tries the back door, and it is locked, the key missing. She goes to the front door, and it too is locked, the key gone. "She was on the verge of trying the windows when she suddenly remembered Sarah. She was afraid for Sarah. Sarah hadn't made a sound in hours."

She rushes to the den and finds Howard polishing away at the same spot, apparently not having moved an inch; yet the phone is on the floor beside him with the wires jerked from the wall.

Sarah, the dog, is in the closet storeroom, dead, and Howard forces Mrs. Gillis in there with her. Later, when he lets her out, the postman, then the milkman come to the door, but Howard stands over Mrs. Gillis with a knife so she dares not cry for help.

In the end, Mrs. Gillis is still alive, but she might not have been. And the dramatic elements have been equally successful in play and story.

We published stories by Langston Hughes, Truman Capote, Stanley Kauffman, Robert Fontaine, William March, Ferenc Molnár, and Saroyan, most of whose plays were produced either just before or soon after their stories appeared in the magazine. There were also Joseph Heller, Ludwig Bemelmans of course, and Robert Ayre, whose "Mr. Sycamore" became a play with Lillian Gish and now, many years later, is being produced as a motion picture. The literary quality of most of these writers is unquestioned, their prose firmly controlled and the plots dramatically constructed. And each author, obviously, had a highly developed feeling for the footlights.

### 3. Practice of Honesty: Clear-Sightedness

Honesty is a kind of energy and strengthens our hand in whatever we may be writing. It comes from the source of what we know, and is not impeded by lies along the way. Honesty is not held back by subterfuge, hobbled by faulty memory of what we may have said or written the day before, does not lead us to a dead end because by following a devious route we lost our way.

One test of the absence of trickery in an author's work is whether the writing itself leaves a conviction that the author can be taken at his word. That we *feel* we may trust him, let him lead us on strange paths, and accept his beliefs unreservedly. Honesty cuts through folderol; it communicates by its simplicity; it demands not only our close attention but our acceptance of the integrity of the talent behind the word.

The writer, on his part, should be deceived only when he chooses to be. Let him look at a pine tree and see a menacing monster if that is the fancy of his imagination; but never let him assert that this pine tree is only a bush, or that it is real when it is plastic, without *his* knowing the difference.

Very early in life the writer must begin to question everything around him, precepts, parents, and motives, including even his own. He must be courageous enough to recognize beauty when he witnesses it, and not be afraid to probe deep into the sources of happiness, tragedy, or love. He must give fully of himself to sensation and form the habit of comparing one impulse or sensation with another, putting all this into words. And if he must write it into bad poetry, even this is good exercise at the beginning.

He must work at self-education—that is, at finding his own truths and convictions—for this is of prime importance to any writer, regardless of any other education he may acquire. Many writers have felt they had not time enough for the lengthy years of a so-called higher education, knowing instinctively how much they had to learn for themselves in that mysterious process of becoming a writer. Without their consciously making a choice, it seemed to have been made for them. Katherine Anne Porter, William Faulkner, Ernest Hemingway—the list is endless of those who found what they needed to know, in life or in literature, from some inner directive of their own. But others, like F. Scott Fitzgerald and Sinclair Lewis, enriched their talents and used their university experiences in their writing. One does not preclude the other.

To sum it up, honesty is clear-sightedness, the habit of seeing clearly, exploring deeply all the motives hidden beneath the surface. Of understanding one's needs and finding for oneself what will strengthen the hand and give validity to one's work as a writer. Honesty is also the practice of *being* truthful, of seeing the truth, and daring at all costs to use it.

### 4. Empathy and Compassion. Understanding

Jean-Paul Sartre says the writer may judge his work or others' by the quality of the writing, but the reader will judge it by the emotions it arouses. George Moore said, "No tears in the writer, no tears in the reader." We ourselves may understand it this way: a writer without sympathy or understanding for his characters or for the human condition would have difficulty arousing emotional response in any reader.

The imaginative person's sympathies are sometimes too easily aroused for remote subjects. Someone must care for mistreated animals on someone else's doorstep, starving children in distant lands, bombed villages he will never see, and maybe send a contribution. A writer, however, has other responsibilities. When he does see and feel something strongly, personally, sympathetically, he must find a way to express this disturbance in his writing, using his sympathy or his sorrow or his delight creatively then or else storing it away in memory for the future. Sometimes far in the future; but eventually most of what the writer feels must come out in his work.

A writer is a person of sensibilities, aware of others; a person of irritations and exaltations and exacerbations, capable of tenderness and, hopefully, of understanding. Trollope observed long ago that before a writer can attract a reader, both sympathy and imagination must be at work; and Joseph Conrad advised a writer to enlarge his sympathies by patient and loving observation while growing in mental power. "A writer without interest or sympathy for the foibles of his fellow man is not conceivable as a writer," he wrote, and empathy, a kind of self-identifying sympathy, a vicarious experiencing of the feelings of another, is a writer's most valued gift. The Random House Dictionary gives us a use for the word: *"By means of empathy a great painting becomes a mirror of oneself."*

What we write ought to be, ideally, the viewpoint of an individual who has truly and imaginatively experienced his own life, who has been aware of his own emotions and the emotions of others, feelingly and significantly. If we cannot weep, laugh, make love with our characters, we will convey little emotion in our writing; our own outlook is what we have to add to the raw material. The reader should come away convinced of the truth of the writer's vision, certain that here is one who has seen, heard, and felt things and reflected on them well.

The writer's task is to know more about his subject and his characters than anyone else could possibly know without his art; to cultivate the wit and empathy to put himself inside friends, enemies, lovers, strangers, striving continually to throw aside all preconceived ideas and prejudices. If the writer is a man, let him write about women honestly, seeing them as individually as his intelligence will allow. If the writer is a woman, let her try to record words a man says, actions he performs, and by her sympathetic feelings about him, let her show the whole man, or at least any part she honestly understands or has honestly observed.

Leave out sentimentality and purely emotional judgments as you would wipe soot from a canvas on which you would paint. Don't make an emotion pretty when it is distasteful, don't add distasteful details in a false attempt to give an appearance of realism. Empathy includes revulsion as well as attraction; it includes any kind of involvement that is used honestly and with acute understanding.

André Gide said, "Often with good sentiments we produce bad literature." Sometimes this is the fault of stories in popular magazines which strive for a form of empathy called "reader identification"—but when it is falsified by pretty endings or self-dramatizing posturing, the reader is being indulged in chocolate marshmallow sundaes when he should be having the fruits of the earth.

Understanding is not always kind or forgiving, but without it we cannot pretend to write knowingly of our fellow man.

### 5. The Fertilizing Senses: Sight, Hearing, Smell, Touch, and Intuition

A writer is alert to his senses. He can see what he looks at, he can hear the talk of others and set it down in convincing prose; he can smell the physical *odeur de pension* along with Balzac, or the scent of the camellias with Proust, the subtler smell of moral decay carried intact onto the stage by Tennessee Williams. He can even say, as Guy de Maupassant told Flaubert, "I have almost finished my Vénus Rustique, and I'd like to . . . her."

It would be difficult to describe anything without drawing on the observation of the senses. To paraphrase an old fable, an elephant could be described by a blind writer (if he held only its trunk) as a reptile that is long and slender and curved upward at one end; by a deaf writer, as having a large mouth out of which there comes no sound. An observing writer with no olfactory sense could say the elephant smells like a rose, and one with no spatial sense, that it is as big as the sky beyond. And a writer with no sense of touch could report that he felt nothing, therefore nothing is there; whereas a writer with no intuition would find no meaning in the elephant's existence.

It is by using all our senses that we comprehend the full values of the physical world, and it is by describing them that we develop the subtleties and poetry of our language.

*Sight* plays a large part in our selection of subject matter in the first place. We *see* a crying child with an upturned sled against a background of winter snow, and our imagination starts to work. Is the child hurt, lost, or only frightened? Will someone come along and find her, and what if no one does?

We *see* a plain schoolteacher past her youth being propelled in a gondola in Venice under a bright, hot sky. We *see* one of her hands, the knuckles too prominent, self-consciously reach down with imitative elegance into the water, her smile too tense as the gondolier leans forward to speak to her. We *see* her say a word in reply but do not hear, and we wonder if anyone has ever made love to her. Is this a story we can imagine?

We *hear* words in a restaurant behind our backs. A young couple is quarreling, and the girl starts to cry audibly. We do not see them and we do not turn around. If we constructed a story from this incident, we would have to rely on the memory of our other senses to fill in more than the sound of their voices. But we have *heard* the quarrel.

Suddenly in the night we *smell* tobacco. We see no one, we have heard no footsteps, but we know we are not alone. Is it a friendly passerby, a thief who would steal our silver, or a young boy hiding, not yet old enough to have the right to smoke? Simenon has started his Maigret novels with nothing more concrete than such awareness.

As for *touch*—we may have known someone for a long time, kept his name in our telephone book, spoken of him casually with friends. Then one day we touch—and there is a message of attraction between us that could change our entire lives. This can be a happy love story, or the beginning of a tragic tale leading to death.

Finally, we know nothing without *intuition,* that sensory and mental gift by which we produce "with the least tangible alloy of extraneous elements" the best work of which we are capable. Abbé Dimnet has said, "Suddenly an illumination flashes upon us which we had perhaps longed for, perhaps not. In one instant we see as the word implies what we had not seen before, and we become conscious of the repose accompanying certitude."

He concludes, "Treat intuitions tenderly," and all serious writers know that there is only one way to bring forth, from the deepest knowledge we have, the thoughts that may illuminate all the rest. It is necessary to listen to the intuition, to let it guide us into ways the conscious mind does not imagine, to reveal to us more than we thought we knew.

The senses belong to all the arts, but it is the particular obligation of the writer to use these gifts to illustrate the whole of life.

## 6. Imagination and a Selective Memory. Reflections, Daydreaming

It is generally agreed that one seldom imagines things from scratch in one's writing. We start with experience, though we may change it all around; we are prompted by characters we have known, characters interpreted by emotions we have had in the past; we use symbols unconsciously chosen and rarely interpreted by ourselves in advance; and we conclude with meanings of some depth—we hope —which give substance to our tales. The result is then called a product of our imagination, and perhaps we should let it go at that; but without a selective memory our creations would lack substance; without imagination a Treasurer's Report of trial and balance would not carry us far.

Henry James says in his indispensable *Notebooks* that one must observe perpetually "the onset of age, another's greed and one's own despondency. . . . Writing is not primarily escape, but use."

If a person or an incident affects you in a particular way, examine that fact, pause, dwell on it. Let that character or that event or thought linger in your mind: taste it, hear it, come to some conclusion about it. Toss these and other scraps in the *pot au feu* of your imagination along with your intuition and other senses, and then decide how you may best serve the result—as a short story, a poem, or a novel, or simply as an anecdote to amuse your friends.

We absorb; we sympathize; we reject; we present; it all comes from our own selective memory in the end.

Someone once advised the writer first to *memorize* his own life; to write from all of it he can remember. If we are sensitive to things others may have missed; if we have kept our interests and experiences fluid as in love, so that we are capable of merging our passions with those of another; if we have developed a memory that is active and reflective, that stores things for later use; and if from childhood on we have hoarded the pleasures of daydreaming—then we need not worry about the well running dry, we will always have material about which to write.

Edward J. O'Brien, founder of the *Best American Short Stories* series, into which he sifted the best published each year in America and Great Britain from 1915 until 1941, decided shortly before his death to warn off would-be writers who lacked the necessary qualities. "If you do not have an alert and curious interest in character and in dramatic situation, if you have no visual imagination and are unable to distinguish between honest emotional reactions and sentimental approaches to life, you will never write a competent short story."

"An alert and curious interest" and "visual imagination" have marked every writer of consequence the world has recorded. Henry James longed, he said, for the audacity to listen at keyholes. In "My Side of the Matter" Truman Capote has a young man peeking between the attic floorboards to satisfy his need to know what his elders and his child-wife are up to in the room below. The imagination is what gives the writer flight, the key to what moves him to become a writer in the first place.

John Dryden wrote: "The first happiness of the poet's imagination is properly invention, or the finding of the thought; the second is fancy, or the variation, deriving, or moulding of that thought."

He might have gone on to name a third stage—when the results of the writer's imagination have convinced the reader of the truth of his daydreaming.

## 7. Love of Language: Words, Phrases, Images

Flaubert wrote to Maupassant: "Whatever you want to say, there is only one [right] word that will express it, one verb to make it move, one adjective to qualify it. You must seek that word, that verb, and that adjective, and never be satisfied with approximations, never resort to tricks, even clever ones, or to verbal pirouettes to escape the difficulty."

Some individuals like to play with golf balls, or trains, or politics. A writer likes to play with words. He is constantly turning his reactions to life into words in order to recall what it was that moved or interested him. Encountering somewhere the phrase "sea-shouldering whales" set Keats off in poetry; Thomas Wolfe said that all his life was a search "to find a word for it [life], a language that would tell its shape, its color, the way we have all known and felt and seen it."

Every writer assumes an obligation to use the language he knows with care and sensitivity and meaningfulness. To put together what "really happened," not as someone else would record it, but as his ear and sensitivity tell him is the only possible way for him to write. And even then he must work constantly to improve on himself, sharpen his awareness of words and their meaning tirelessly and lovingly. A writer must be forever studying and learning his language as he would a foreign tongue, for meaning, for vocabulary, for subtleties and inflection.

The poet Marianne Moore said, "Words cluster like chromosomes, determining procedure." And again, "A man is a writer if all his words are strung on definite recognizable sentence sounds." The sounds come to us by ear, but we must transfer the words onto paper in order to produce sound again in the reader's mind.

To Sartre, "poetry creates the myth, the prose writer draws its portrait." He goes on to say that for the writer language is the structure of the external world. "He maneuvers words from within; he feels them as if they were his body. . . . In short, all language is for him the mirror of the world. The word tears the writer of prose away from himself and throws him in the midst of the world."

It is through language that we communicate best and most easily. But also, sometimes, most disastrously. Thought must come before words, although the writer has a special privilege: he may change his words, improve on them, edit and reduce them when he has said too much. If we find we have not made our meaning clear, if we have buried the substance of our thought in too much verbiage, we may rearrange, substitute the "one word that will express it," that "one adjective to qualify it." The writer need not be read before he is ready.

In the beginning (and always thereafter, of course), the writer must observe exact rules for the uses of words, for grammar, for the principles of composition. One must be sharply aware of words misused, avoiding verbose writing and clichés both in phrases and in our thinking. The best dictionary one can afford must always be close by, and such books as *The Elements of Style,* by William Strunk, Jr., and E. B. White, are indispensable.

To further sensitize your ear to your own use of language, it is valuable to read your work aloud, even to yourself. Avoid awkwardness in expression, but avoid glibness with equal care. There should be a sort of rhythm of thought in structure, particularly in paragraphing, but a singing rhythm does not belong in prose that has something of substance to say. Prose relates to the heartbeat, as do most satisfactory expressions of an art, but in meaning and vitality, not in poetry.

Avoid fancy verbs, but use active ones when possible.

Use several adjectives for conscious effect; or use none at all, extending your descriptions with a phrase. One adjective must be used with the utmost care, after rejecting those that are less effective.

Use adverbs with discretion, and never try to invent your own.

Read poetry to sharpen your sense of metaphor; history to bring you down to the realities of Fate; biography and psychology to add to your knowledge of human behavior; and great fiction to renew your feeling for the meaning and possibilities of life.


## 8. Style; Wit; Irony

"Style," said Robert Frost, "is less the man than the way a man takes himself." It is the coat of many colors he puts on when he appears in public, and if it fits him and shows off his figure, it is his coat. Sometimes it is borrowed by those who think they can wear it as well, but they would have done better had they taken their own measurements first.

*Style* is basic in the total expression of man. It is in the rhythm of his speech, the expression in his eyes, and the nature of his responses to emotion or thought. Or to life or death. It is also a test of a writer's powers of observation and the flexibility of his vocabulary.

In *The Elements of Style* E. B. White wrote, "There is no satisfactory explanation of style, no infallible guide to good writing, no assurance that a person who thinks clearly will be able to write clearly, no key that unlocks the door, no inflexible rules by which the young writer may shape his course. He will often find himself steering by stars that are disturbingly in motion."

The truism is that the best style is the least noticeable, the manner which least stands in the way of matter presented. Samuel Butler said he could not conceive how any author could think about style without loss to himself and his readers. He did not know, he said, in the end whether he wrote with "style" or not. It was to him just "common, simple straightforwardness."

Balzac had a rule: "Be clear." If he was not clear, he said, his world of fiction crumbled. Hemingway's style was clear, "the one intrinsic style our century has produced," wrote Archibald Mac-Leish. By "chiseling away surplusage," he attained a classicism of line in his prose. Faulkner, who wanders in and out of a veritable jungle of tone-setting words and images, has a style which translates well in many languages.

Robert Louis Stevenson, however, believed that the most perfect style "is not, as the fools say, that which is most natural, for the most natural is the disjointed babbling of the chronicler; but that which attains the highest degree of elegant and pregnant implication unobtrusively; if obtrusively, then with the greatest gain to sense and vigor."

Style, which is one of the elements that make the writer unique and the reading of his work most interesting, will be spoken of more fully in a later chapter.

*Wit* is essential in a writer, a lover, a talker, or a doer. It is wit —that ability to juxtapose one thought on another to unexpectedly sharpen our responses, to bring recognition and frequently delight —which is at the root of all truly effective drama and literature. From Molière to Tennessee Williams we have these unexpected moments which astonish, intrigue, and complete our own sense of the incongruities of the world around us.

Jean Cocteau has said, "The spirit of creation is the spirit of contradiction. It is the breakthrough of appearances toward an unknown reality."

Wit is the ability to draw conclusions that may totally surprise. It startles, amuses, and is most effective when subtle and unannounced.

Wit in literature is the ability to conclude a thought arrestingly, a phrase significantly, and a story successfully. Wit is the capacity to see the ridiculous, to recognize the essence of behavior, and to recall incongruities.

*Irony* represents again the unexpected truths we hope to bring to light; the ability to see conclusions which may be as contradictory and as incongruous as life itself. Irony must be inherent in the situation, probably the reverse of what has been expected. Dramatic irony is defined in the dictionary as an effect achieved by making the audience aware of something a character or participant does not know. A short story almost always achieves its effect by means of irony.

Irony is never far from the thinking of fiction writers. The absurdities of life, of good and evil, of protestations and hypocrisy and actions and avoidances—all this is the stuff to stimulate one's story sense and to provide drama in the written tale.

## 9. Regularity and Capacity for Work: Pursuit of Excellence

We can do no better than to quote other writers on work: its regularity, its abundance, its difficulties in the face of a writer's growing, or perhaps dwindling, capacities. Prolonged and concentrated labor is a necessity that all successful writers understand. Work is that hard rock of reality that separates writer from wisher, that mountain which must be mounted again and again and conquered before a writer can claim the view on the other side as his own.

E. M. Forster worked out a novelist's schedule this way: sleep eight hours, eat two hours, love two hours, and spend one hour a day on church or God. The rest of the time would be spent at his desk.

Mary O'Hara, who wrote *My Friend Flicka* nine times, gets up earlier and earlier in the mornings as a book progresses. Edna Ferber wrote steadily from nine to four every day.

All writers have heard somewhere or other that Balzac had a horrendous routine. Two weeks to two months were spent on a book. During this time he went to bed at eight after a light dinner with white wine; he awoke and was back at his desk by 2 A.M., where he then wrote until six, drinking coffee from a pot kept permanently on the stove. At six he took a bath for an hour, then drank more coffee until his publisher came with proofs and took away corrected ones from the day before and new manuscript pages. From nine until twelve he wrote again, then breakfasted on eggs and more coffee. From one until six he worked at corrections.

When a book was done he then saw friends or mistresses, or disappeared from sight.

Simenon, after checking on his health with his physician, carves out a piece of his life for each new book. And for the necessary period of writing time he claims to give up family, social life, and all other diversions, working almost around the clock until the book is done.

Southey said, "By writing much, one learns to write well." And so it goes. Each writer must eventually settle on his own best pattern of production: the hours in which the imagination is better controlled, the period of the day when uninterrupted work is most possible.

Superficial interruptions are bad enough—the ringing of the phone, a duty to perform, a review to be done—but the larger interruptions, in which forces vital to writing well are used, can be fatal. One cannot give one's *best* to any other job and have creative energy left over for writing.

This point has been argued frequently, of course. Some publishers have been known to suggest that an author short of money "get a job" to finish a book. Some would-be writers go into the teaching profession, or editing, or journalism, thinking in this way to keep in touch with the subject in which they are most vitally interested. It won't work. Better to chop down trees, cook dinners, drive a taxi, or go hunting or fishing—anything with no carryover is safest, once you know where your true interest lies.

Oliver LaFarge observed that "man after man gives it up and turns aside; the ones who stay with it have the guts."

Accept the premise that writing requires not only long hours of concentrated effort, but also a tough hide to repel the darts of family and friends who wish we would keep the same conventional hours and values as the rest of the human race. An author must also be able to put things aside when work is done; to refrain from talking about his writing to the point of boring everyone, including his professional peers *and* his wife; to try, when the demon is *not* upon him, to live and love and laugh and share, to recover a vulnerability to persons and desires not invented first by himself.

There are three stages of work for most writers, and the time spent on each varies with the individual.

First, there is the gathering of material, the daydreaming and contemplation of an idea that has taken root in the imagination. This is sometimes a waiting period in which the subjects that will assemble and become fictional substance develop an energy of their own. The theme develops in the writer's mind, and characters take the shape and physical reality they will have in a story or a novel, although at this stage some are more clearly seen than others. This period is long or short, depending on the method of work or on the complexity of the idea.

John Toldy, Academy Prize–winning author and collaborator with Whit on *The Love Story of Robert Burns,* used to walk in Central Park for hours each night and morning, actually writing his stories in his head. He composed with such concentration that rarely would a word be changed once he started the physical task of putting it all down on paper. Somerset Maugham also worked things out in detail before the actual writing and warned against setting down impressions "in their original vagueness."

The second stage is the actual writing, and some writers do prefer to sit down at their typewriters when the feel of a story, but sometimes little else, is there. D. H. Lawrence first felt his stories in his solar plexus, and then let things happen as the story went along. Many writers speak of the sense that the story is all written in some part of their imaginations before they start, and the process of writing is then more like reading a page than inventing a story. True it is that once a story or novel is under way, the writing time shortens and the periods of indecision decrease; apparently there is only one right way to do a thing if only it can be found, and the better the focus, the clearer becomes our direction.

All writers find delight in the surprises characters or plots spring on them from time to time. The original plot outline may still be followed, but it is only the hack writer who cannot see beyond a prearranged scheme. Robert Frost spoke of his own "stumble and recovery method," the joy of discovering his exact meaning as he went along. The important thing for a writer is to lose himself in the story at every stage of development, and to remain immersed until the end in the pleasures of his creation.

The third stage is the rewriting, or self-editing, or simply reworking, which may take as long, or ten times as long, as the first and second stages together. Sometimes, after the first quick but concentrated writing is done, it is better to put the work aside for a time. Katherine Anne Porter started her *Ship of Fools* many times in different versions before the final work took shape. Peter Benchley, author of the best-selling novel *Jaws,* says he studied the habits of sharks and had the idea for a novel fifteen years before the book was written.

Sometimes one starts to write a book too early, before the characters and plot have been well defined or clearly differentiated. Sometimes the theme has not yet been intelligently articulated, and one may end with a conglomeration of aims, having taken off in too many directions.

Or one may start too late, when one's research and interest in the material have taken so long that the original impulse has been exhausted.

When is the best time to begin, once the original thought has come upon us? Think, daydream, ponder for a time—but not too long. Put down a note in a journal, direct the subconscious to fasten on any reference to the subject from any source—never let the idea escape completely from your mind. For example, once the idea for *Jaws* came into Peter Benchley's head, all that was known on the subject began to fascinate him, he says, to accrete around his original conception, until writing the novel was an act of unavoidable compulsion.

A writer's work is always difficult for the nonwriter to understand. We seem to be idle at hours when others are at work, and although many of us do go to our desks at an appointed time each day and clock off a predetermined number of pages, not all writers' minds work in this orderly fashion. Continuing performance is absolutely essential—allowing respite for those periods when the brain is depleted from its labor—but each of us knows, after a fashion, how best we will produce our most satisfactory work, and that, more often than not, regularity does matter.

For others, who must wait until the spell is upon them and then work as much as eight or ten hours a day until a thing is done, another sort of discipline seems to be necessary. Simenon, of whom we spoke earlier, has long nonwriting periods, then plunges into a book full force. Saroyan wrote more than a hundred stories a year when he began to have success, but appears less often today. Sometimes a writer appears in print too often and earns the name of a hack. It is hard to take seriously the ideas of a writer who will turn out too many novels a year, unless he is a Simenon, and perhaps he too now has somewhat surfeited his market, so that a certain degree of our expectancy is lost.

Joseph Conrad said writing is torture, and it is all too often the end of a writer's endurance that stops his working day. The necessity for prolonged concentration, prolonged feeling, prolonged execution and artistic control of one's material is obvious; yet our attention span is only so long, our love or anger or compassion toward our characters, as in life, cannot remain at high pitch indefinitely. One must also know when to stop, and when to begin again.

Whatever the working habits, whatever the achievement, there is one important bit of advice all writers must heed. "Be there when the writing is going on," said Marianne Moore, and get it on the page.

## 10. Talent; Audacity. A Touch of Genius

Talent is easily discerned in the young. A feeling for music and the gift of execution are unmistakable and not uncommon. The sense of color and the feeling for form that mark the painter show up in a child at a young age. A love of words, a gift for speech, and a devotion to reading should indicate the future writer. Unfortunately writing success does not always follow.

This apparent talent, this trying out of possibilities—is it a passing thing until the gifted person goes on to something else, or is it merely imitative, a form of glibness, a desire to please and be praised?

*Talent,* as Flaubert said, *is a long patience.*

Curiously, the signs of writing talent may be deceptive. In the examination of a writer's gifts and promise, it is not always easy to see where this actually exists, or where talent may be developed. Some musicians, after one course of training, find they have then a marvelous left hand that can fly over the fingerboard of a fiddle in all positions and with fine effect. They may not, however, adequately develop the bow arm.

In the writer, says Trollope, both sympathy and imagination must be at work before a writer can attract a reader. One must also have something to say: pretty phrases, even an impressive vocabulary, do not always indicate talent in the writer. An ability to tell a story may. The need to say something in a particular way, to convince, to interest, even by means of nonliterary language, will more often than not lead one to a writer who will become important in the literary world.

It was not easy at *STORY* to explain what we were looking for. Agents who sent us short stories often made the error of submitting simply fine writing they could not sell to the commercial magazines, telling us that here would be "the originality you are looking for." Originality has no place if it remains merely chaotic, and fine writing is a bore if it has no story to tell or communicates nothing.

The first stories of Truman Capote and Norman Mailer were neither fine writing nor chaotic. "My Side of the Matter," by Truman, and "The Greatest Thing in the World," by Norman, were tightly written stories with plot and character. One had humor, the other had imaginative substance; and each had vitality, a story, and economy of language.

Does a writer write for himself, for others, or maybe for money? It doesn't matter if the talent is there. Talent is not as corruptible as may be believed, but it can be misguided and wasted. For economic reasons it can be used up on slick writing, for which the market seems happily dwindling; it can be delayed in journalism; or be dissipated by writing in other media where even a unique gift may be dishearteningly taken for granted.

*Courage* is needed to keep on writing one's best, or better, or even to keep writing at all. Sherwood Anderson wrote to a friend in February 1939: "I find, Gilbert, that many of the young artists who from time to time come to see me are too full of a kind of self-pity. The cruelty and indifference of so much of life amazes them too much. There is, I guess, a kind of final test, to take it *laughing*. There is a kind of maturity in that."

*Audacity. Toujours l'audace* has been a motto for other than military geniuses. Artists in advance of their times have emblazoned it in their work, and if they live long enough, it has well repaid them. Audacity is sometimes nothing more than the unshakable conviction that your own point of view is sound and your methods are right; that, and having the courage to stick to it, with conviction. An artist without audacity or conviction may be pushed from manner to manner, method to method, and never make the necessary discoveries of his own talent in his work. Conviction makes itself manifest primarily by its independence. An artist having fun, tossing up and playing with his subject and abilities—as Dali and Picasso have done —may puzzle us by his shifts and starts, his many flights and moods. But each has had the audacity to enjoy his divagations, his self-expression, and the particular vision he has of life.

It also takes audacity to fail and keep right on with what you intend to do. Chekhov's first plays were panned, and yet he continued writing for the comic magazines, and practicing medicine, not once giving up his plans for a literary success. Joyce's book of short stories was banned in his native land; Sherwood Anderson's first short stories each brought him no more than $25; and Henry Miller reached middle age before the work of his youth was known outside his own Parisian circle. But their persistence confirms the virtue of audacity.

Coleridge said it when his *Lyrical Ballads* was new and creating opposition: "Every great and original writer, in proportion as he is great or original must himself create the taste by which he is to be relished."

And for writers who may have doubts, Dr. Ernest Jones, disciple of that literature-affecting genius of his day, Dr. Sigmund Freud, says there is a little trace of genius in nearly everyone.

"Genius," as he defined it, "is not a quality, but only a quantitative

difference in a combination of attributes contained in all persons."
Those attributes are as follows:

1. Inspiration
2. Spontaneity
3. Periodicity or cycles of production
4. Absolute honesty
5. Regularity
6. A sense of significance
7. Concentration.

There is no harm in accepting this definition, but let us also read Sydney Smith, wit and clergyman of the nineteenth century, who describes "genius" thus:

"The meaning of an extraordinary man is that he is eight men, not one man; that he has as much wit as if he had not sense, and as much sense as if he had no wit; that his conduct is as judicious as if he were the dullest of human beings, and his imagination as brilliant as if he were irretrievably ruined."

Good writers of the genius class are welcomed.

# II
# ELEMENTS OF FICTION

# 1
# PLOTTING AND
# NARRATIVE DEVELOPMENT

As WHIT ONCE said in discussing plotting with his students: "Forster
defines a story as 'a narrative of events in their time sequences.' And
so Sinbad went here and there and somewhere else and this happened to him, etc. It is a chronology—itinerary. A straight narrative
of what happened. A plot is what you do with that story. It is your
plan of arranging the events, not necessarily in a time sequence, but
in an artistic sequence—in a selective sequence. He defines plot as
narrative of events with the emphasis falling on causality—on the
reason, on the *why* these events happened. He gives a good example: the king died and the queen died. That is a simple story. Two
facts, one following another. Maybe that is a story and maybe just
a couple of facts. It has no arrangement. Just tells the truth and there
you are. If there is one more element added to these two facts you
might get a plot. What would that element be?"

Student: "You might say the queen died of a broken heart."

W. B.: "Practically a perfect answer. You could have a cause for
both of their deaths; but it would not be a buildup. In the beginning
they are perfectly happy. But the king dies and then the queen dies
of grief. That is a plot. As the result of one fact, another fact happens.
The time sequence is still preserved, but the sense of *why* overshad-
ows the time sequence, so you become interested in why the queen
died. Now, if you wanted to make it a little more complicated, how
would you do that?"

Student: "Have the queen far away and returning home—"

W. B.: "Good. We add geography. The king in Cairo. The queen
in China. This adds an element of background which will enrich the
story somewhat—but not much. It is still all a little silly. Like some

slick writers. They take dummies and throw them about in situation after situation and hope something jells. That is not the way we want to write short stories.

"No, let's have the queen die. *No one knows why.* That starts your story off at this moment. You don't have the deathbed scene of the king. The queen dies and although the king has also just died, no one connects the two at first—because the queen had always been a lady who fancied a knight or two so nobody guessed how much she'd loved the king. Somebody then has to investigate, unravel the causes of the queen's mysterious death; and now you have suspense. Complicate the plot by having the knight, her lover, not wanting *his* wife to know. How do they try to prevent the investigation? And those who want to preserve the queen's good name, how do they scramble to cover it all up? But no, the queen *has* died of grief, we said at the beginning, and here is our chance to develop a nice psychological story. Instead of the tum, tum, tum of event, event, event, it is a problem to be solved, a mystery to be revealed and brought to some conclusion.

"What you have now is that the plot of your story—the action of your characters, plus a selection on your part to emphasize the connection or the relationships to show why—is revealing *something.*"

Plot then, we say, is an arrangement of related events establishing a situation, with anticipation, suspense, emotion, and satisfaction in a dramatic form. Aristotle simplified the whole thing by saying that plot is the *arrangement* of incidents—incidents which "must be whole, complete in themselves, and of adequate importance."

Somerset Maugham has said that it is only through plotting that an author gratifies the desire of the reader to know what happens to people in whom one's interest has been aroused.

Finally, Webster's dictionary defines plot as "a plot devised to entrap others."

It is difficult to arouse our interest in a work of fiction without also stirring our curiosity and our interest in what happens next. Related incidents, each either building onto or contradicting another, must carry the reader from page to page, and the greater the author's agility, the less resistance a reader will have to continue with his tale. To return to Aristotle, we keep reading in hopes of coming to a conclusion both "inevitable and unexpected."

Plot is closely connected with style, which means that dramatic arrangement of a story's parts may vary widely with the individual writer's own rhythm and view of life.

Stephen Crane's "The Open Boat, Being the Experience of Four Men from the Sunk Steamer *Commodore,*" simply presents the problem of how these men fight to save themselves from the sea. It is full of action, and we know from the beginning the men's state of mind and their plight.

"None of them knew the color of the sky. Their eyes glanced level, and were fastened upon the waves that swept toward them. These waves were of the hue of slate, save for the tops, which were of foaming white, and all of the men knew the colors of the sea. The horizon narrowed and widened, and dipped and rose, and at all times its edge was jagged with waves that seemed thrust up in points like rocks.

"Many a man ought to have a bathtub larger than the boat which here rode upon the sea."

We are introduced to the characters: the cook, whose "sleeves were rolled over his fat forearms, and the two flaps of his unbuttoned vest dangled as he bent to bail out the boat"; the oiler, "steering with one of the two oars in the boat"; the correspondent, "pulling at the other oar, watched the waves and wondered why he was there"; and the injured captain, lying in the bow.

The author tells us, "A singular disadvantage of the sea lies in the fact that after successfully surmounting one wave you discover that there is another behind it just as important, and just as nervously anxious to do something effective in the way of swamping boats."

After bailing and rowing and despairing, the captain pointed to "a small, still thing on the edge of the swaying horizon. It was precisely like the point of a pin. It took an anxious eye to find a lighthouse so tiny."

The men worked together with new hope, obedient to the captain, feeling "the subtle brotherhood of men that was here established on the seas." And slowly the land rose from the sea, trees and sand. Then the lighthouse.

For a time they saw no one on land, and the force of the sea kept driving them back. "If this old ninny-woman, Fate, cannot do better than this, she should be deprived of the management of men's fortunes," the narrator comments. "If she has decided to drown me, why did she not do it in the beginning and save me all this trouble?"

The tide changed and the men were near exhaustion. Rowing, "suddenly there was another swish and another long flash of bluish light, and this time it was alongside the boat, and might almost have been reached with an oar. The correspondent saw an enormous fin speed like a shadow through the water, hurling the crystalline spray and leaving the long glowing trail." The shark did not leave until dawn.

They were still headed for the shore as "the monstrous inshore rollers heaved the boat high until the men were again enabled to see the white sheets of water scudding up the slanted beach. " 'Now, remember to get well clear of the boat when you jump,' said the captain."

In the water, swimming, paddling, struggling, three of the men made it to shore. In the end, though, "in the shallows, face downward, lay the oiler," and he was no longer alive.

Every word of this story advances the plot, sustains the suspense, the promise, and the question is answered: Will the men be saved? The men are saved.

Chekhov's short story "The Darling" has another sort of plot, a simple one, basing its interest not on contradiction but on assent; indeed, it is this very element of plodding agreement in the story line that is the surprise. We expect some turn or twist, but the final irony, the power of this plot, is that we *should have* expected the way it ends, but because of the author's skill, we did not.

The central character, a young wife, married and became her husband's darling; he died and she married again and was the same adoring wife to the second husband. She went through a lifetime of too easy compliance—with each change in her fortunes not changing her, as the reader expects—simply taking on the colors and desires of the man she marries. In the end, having been the darling of three men, she became so habituated to her role that even when she was left with nothing more than a schoolboy, she became a "darling" to him.

A tightly plotted story with unexpected twists is Norman Mailer's "The Greatest Thing in the World," which won our College Prize when the author was only eighteen, a student at Harvard, and not at all certain of a future in literature. This was his first published story and even then indicated that footlight sense we spoke of earlier.

Al Groot, his character, was also eighteen, away from home and

broke. He got a ride with three tough guys into Chicago, and reck-
lessly challenged one to a game of pool—which he'd played just
three times before in his life. Fortunately, his opponent, Pickles,
wasn't much good either, and Al began winning most of Pickle's
money. And he wanted to keep it.

"Pickles stroked his cue, grinning. 'Your luck's been too good,
sweet-face. I think this is going to be my game. I got twenty bucks
left. I'm laying it down.'

" 'No,' said Al. 'I don't want to.'

" 'Listen, I been losing dough. You're playing.'

"They all looked at him menacingly."

Al saw there was no escape and also knew he couldn't win. He
put down his cue.

" 'Where you going?' asked Pickles.

" 'To the can. Want to come along?' He forced a laugh from the
very bottom of his throat."

In the toilet he saw only one exit, a window high up on the wall.
He boosted himself up and pulled the window open, only to find a
grating above his head. He couldn't escape there, so he hid the
money in the crotch of his pants and unlocked the door. The men
were waiting for him and forced him into their car. "Take him out
on the road where no one will hear. . . ."

Al sat there silently, but when the car slowed down at a curve, "his
elbow kicked the door open, and he yanked his hand loose, whirled
about and leaped out, the door just missing him in its swing back."

He escaped, had a full meal and cigarettes, and found a room for
the night. Lying there thinking of all he'd accomplished, "he
stopped, suddenly, unable to continue, so great was his ecstasy. He
lay over his pillow and addressed it.

" 'By God,' Al Groot said, about to say something he had never
uttered before. 'By God, this is the happiest moment of my life.' "

Here is not the brilliantly allusive writing, with its flashing images
and powerful style, we associate with Norman's fiction—indeed with
all his writing—in its maturity, but it is ample evidence of a gifted
mind already oriented in observation of character, in the paradoxes
of life, and in the requirements of plot.

It is interesting also to observe that many of the younger writers
we published who went on to greater success, did not, at the beginning, write the delicate and sensitive unplotted stories of adolescence, but turned away from themselves to objectify experience and

emotion, and even to entertain the reader, in their observations on the social scene.

Too often young writers believe that a sensitized state of mind is enough for a story. That is enough for a state of mind, but that's about all. Since all fiction must have some narrative interest, underuse of plot can be a defect. All editors have felt hope, in beginning a story written well and even arrestingly, only to find it comes to nothing in the end. We then send the story back, and sometimes on rejection slips we write, "Too slight." And the author never seems to know what we mean!

It is also disastrous, of course, to overuse plot. In these cases the author has so proscribed the actions of his characters and the clues by which the story is to be told, that if you cannot guess what is going to happen in the end, it is because you don't know your formula. These classical boy-meets-girl stories are so dominated by the author's overuse of plot (and underuse of sensitivity and sophistication) that after a game of tennis the reader knows they will fall in love and marry, because that is the conventional progress from one point to another. Oh, there will be complications along the way, elaborately conceived and contrived, but the ball of the plot bounces back and forth as in a game of ping-pong played by energetic players.

But not stumbling, of course. We will still have books such as *Love Story*, written by Erich Segal, with the surefootedness of promotional success, and those of Jacqueline Susann, whose books are of value to the intent writer only because of their sentimentality, which he will be increasingly determined to avoid at any cost.

A plot may develop from something which interests us, a character, a situation, or an idea. It always has some element of suspense in it, and the true tale-tellers know the art and artifice of keeping listeners absorbed: when interest is high in the plot, they spin it out, but know the exact moment when the planted gun will go off. Suspense is not only Chekhov's gun, which once put on the table will be expected to be used; it can also be a subtle complicity with the reader, that half-revealed something that makes us ask for more.

In a plot, only the author is in command, able to ravel or unravel at will, encouraging a reader to think he sees the pattern and what is developing, and then perhaps catching him unawares. Yet only the author should know, before the reader, where the story will lead. Without a plot, we could no doubt settle it for the reader all at once, perhaps with a simple explanation; but explanation is not literature.

We want a greater approximation of the truth than that, and in all fiction, what is not explained explicitly must be hinted at by indirection, implication, suggestion—by what is never really told but only indicated. With the reader's participation likely to be working with the author, but not ahead of him, the author will devise his plot.

Writers who say they have trouble with plots are frequently individuals who also say they have trouble with people, with understanding why and how anyone acts the way he does. Henry James points out that Turgenev's plots always sprang from character; he never tired of studying people, and the origin of his plots was almost always the "vision of some person or persons who hovered before him, soliciting him," until he could find the "right relations." Until he could "imagine, invent and select and piece together the situations most useful and favorable in the sense of the creatures themselves, and the complications they would be most likely to produce and to feel." Then, said Turgenev, he would have arrived at his story.

While there is no end to the plots one may devise intellectually —and there are even "plot cards" for hack writers who take the easy way—a plot line is convincing only when the writer is himself convinced that the way his story moves is the only right direction for it to take. He cannot cheat in this any more than in anything else in the writing game.

*Where do we find our plots?* The best plots, and perhaps the only truly valid ones, come from development or revelations in the nature of character. All too often failure in a book or story comes from the author's own superficial understanding, his own lack of sympathy in depth. The great plotters—Dostoevski, Shakespeare, Chaucer, or any other giant of literature—understand that actions must come from an author's following the labyrinthine turns and twistings of fate and of life itself.

Colette, a fine, if less important writer, has brilliantly demonstrated in her fiction the natural and intricate relationships between the characters of whom she writes (more often than not, herself) and the development of these persons into plotted stories, simply by careful exploration of them as individuals.

A plot is not always clearly defined by the author when he begins the labor of his work, and need not be, if he has observed enough and has confidence in his own inner sense of form. The successful writer of Gothic novels, Phyllis Whitney, has said that sometimes she just "puts something in the hopper," which in itself may set her mind pursuing a plot. If then a story "comes into focus," she works it out in detail; the impetus, she says, is often simply that she has been interested in a character "who wants something."

Sometimes an author will take an event of the day and use his imagination to make a story from that. If he has been moved by the event, or intrigued, or angered or disturbed, and if he knows enough about the subject, he may be successful. Yet there are dangers to this method. Even if the story is successful, publication may come after the public has tired of it; or your own feelings and experiences could slant such a story with such bias that the necessary effect—the one you are hoping for—will be spoiled.

A story that used a contemporary event with passion and verisimilitude and a leavening of irony at the end was Michael Thelwell's "The Organizer," which won first prize in *STORY'S* 1969 College Contest. No better record could be found of some tragic moments of the civil rights movement in the South, with an entirely modern twist at the end.

Briefly, it is about a young Northern "agitator" for the Freedom Movement who experiences the full force of white revenge on the black, protesting community, "in the town of Boque Chitto, Mississippi. All of importance is east of the river—the jail, the drugstore and Western Union, the hotel, the Greyhound station, and the Confederate Memorial in the tree-shaded part. West of the river one comes to a paper mill, a cemetery, a junkyard which merges with a garbage dump, and the Negro community.

"Perched on a rise overlooking the dump and cemetery to one side and the Negro shacks on the other side is the Freedom House. . . ."

The "organizer" of the title, Travis Peacock, is in the "unpainted concrete structure with a huge storefront window" waiting for the obscene phone call that comes each night. The black community is increasingly worried, because two staff members are in Atlanta for a meeting, and they feel that Peacock should not be in Freedom House alone. There is always the chance the anger behind the phone calls might be put into action, that someone might be killed.

The call comes just as Travis is falling asleep.

"Knowed yo' wasn't sleepin', Nigger. Ain't nevah goin' sleep no mo'."

Travis waits, but as nothing more happens than has happened any other night, he goes back to sleep. Until he is awakened by "the heavy, somehow ponderous boom of dynamite. Silence, then a yapping, howling chorus as every dog in town began to bark."

Two friends come for Peacock, and the three run toward the explosion in the Negro quarter, to find it has destroyed most of the house in which he has been staying. The family living there was "close as his own kin." Travis runs around the house to the back door. The smell of burnt powder is strong.

The kitchen is filled with people. Mama Jean turns to the door and sees him.

" 'Oh, Travis, Travis, honey. They done hit him. They done kilt Jesse!' The people gave a low moan of assent. It seemed to Travis that they were looking at him accusingly, the stranger who brought death among them."

The story continues as the sheriff and his men, suspicious of Travis and fearful of the anger of the blacks, come into the house as Travis tries to comfort Jesse's wife, Miss Vickie.

"His limbs felt heavy as though he were moving through some heavy liquid medium, but his footsteps sounded loud. He bent and took her hands. They were limp at first, then they imprisoned his in a quick fierce grip. He was looking into her eyes for some sign of warmth, life, recognition, but most of all for some sign of absolution, forgiveness. . . ."

Travis's guilt for the thing he has brought on these people he has come to love almost paralyzes him, and what he sees as the veiled antagonism of the blacks is obvious. Sheriff Hollowell, aware of this, tries to arouse the people against Travis; but their anger is stronger against the white community. The lawmen's fingers are tighter on their guns.

It is then that Travis, himself frightened and grieving, steps before them all and urges the blacks to return peacefully to their homes.

"The skin of his back crawled, sensitive to the slightest pressure of his shirt and waiting for the first probing touch of Hollowell's bullet. He closed his eyes and waited for the crowd's attention."

Reluctantly the blacks listen, but it is only when Travis dares make fun of Hollowell and sets the crowd laughing, finally cheering, that their attention is diverted from their anger and the shock of the tragedy.

" 'He scared lak a girl,' Peacock shouted and forced himself to laugh. 'Why ol bad-assed Bo Hollowell standin' theah shaking jes' lak a dawg trying to shit a peach stone.' That cracked the people up, real laughing, vindictive and punitive to the lawmen, but full, deep and therapeutic to the crowd."

There is a spirited exchange between Travis and the crowd, until finally Travis calls on the Uncle Tom-ish preacher Battle to pray for the victims: and shames the lawmen into bowing their heads and removing their Stetson hats during the prayer.

When it is over and everyone has gone home, Travis returns to Freedom House. He must telephone north and report on the tragedy to the organization, so they may see where it can be used to the advantage of the Cause. But Travis thinks, "So we become shapers of horror, artists of grief, giving form and shape and articulation to emotion, the same emotion, doing it so often that finally there is nothing left of that emotion but the form."

He reports on the situation, hears his superior's plans to use the press, national TV, all information media, getting them to the scene of the tragedy; until finally he cries: "You want to stage a circus. I can't let the family subject themselves to that!"

But money must be raised for Jesse's family and for the Cause; and the Cause is what Travis has been fighting for. In the end he agrees, and says, "Freedom!" before he hangs up.

He even "crossed over to the door, opened it, and stood looking down on the sleeping town. Later today it would be over-run. Camera crews, reporters, photographers, dignitaries. Across the country guilty and shocked people would be writing to Congressmen. Some would reach for checkbooks. . . .

"Peacock sat down and shook his head. He passed his hands over his face, massaging his eyes. He shook his head again. This was a family he loved."

Then he begins to think: "When morning came he would have to go back to be with the family. Funny he hadn't thought of it before, but Miss Vickie had a great face. Be great on a poster, or on TV. . . ."

A very wise story, and sad, written by a student at Howard University at that time, making excellent and dramatic use of contemporary events.

Plot may come from a mood, as Henry James has so masterfully shown. We examine his methods in his own *Notebooks*.

"In order to create a sense of evil," he suggests, "it is first neces-

sary to make the reader's general vision of evil intense enough.
. . . Then his own experience, his imagination, and his sympathy and
revulsion will supply him with the reactions the author's mood must
evoke."

"Make him think the evil," writes James, *"make him think it for
himself."* Thus in *The Turn of the Screw* a reader's complicity with the
evil governess and chauffeur has endured and will endure as long
as the tale is read.

Plot must create strong suspense: if a promise is made a promise
must be kept. We must want to know what will happen next.

There is one type of plotting we haven't touched on yet, which
goes back to P. G. Wodehouse's statement that one shouldn't try to
be literary with a popular story, or try to jazz up popular appeal in
a literary tale. Something like that.

There is, however, something to be said for the story that is fun
to write, intellectually amusing to plot, and happily rewarding in its
success with a reader who wants to be amused above all else. This
is the idea plot, in which outrageous twists and turns can be developed deadpan, characters are superficial but hopefully witty, and the
ultimate aim is to surprise and startle the reader.

"The Ubiquitous Wife" by Marcel Aymé, translated by Whit
Burnett, is a fine example of this genre. It begins:

"Once, in Montmartre, in the rue de l'Abreuvoir, there lived a
young woman by the name of Sabina, who possessed the gift of
ubiquity. Whenever she wished, she was able to multiply herself and
be at the same time, in body and in spirit, in as many places as she
wished."

Sabina keeps this gift from her husband, except that once by
accident he comes upon her multiplying herself before a mirror. He
decides there is something wrong with him and a doctor agrees: *he*
has a glandular deficiency.

When Sabina takes an artist lover, Théorème, having divided
herself in two, her husband is pleased to see frequently a look of
happiness on her face at odd moments as she sits in a room beside
him. He is not aware that she is at that moment making love with
another man.

This life satisfies Sabina for a time, but when Théorème needs
more money than she can give him by the sale of her jewels, she
divides again and becomes the wife of an earl. She then sends money
to Théorème which he squanders on other women and drink. When

Sabina the First finds out about this—she is still living with a contented husband—she repents, refusing to have anything more to do with Théorème. He then, repentant and broke, does become a successful artist, but Sabina, overwhelmed "in expiation of the life of deceit she has lived with her good husband, Antoine Lemutier," divides herself for the last time. Incidentally, for various reasons, she has been divided by now into 56,000 selves.

Sabina begins a life of penance under the name of Louise Mégnin in a shack of scrap lumber and tarpaper. In a room "filled with filth and rats," she is raped one day by a monstrous-looking man "built like a gorilla in the breadth of his shoulders" when he forces his way into her shack. He returns a day or so later with a sack of pâté de foie gras, smoked salmon, twelve bottles of red wine, a bottle of rum, and various other goodies, and doesn't leave until five o'clock two days later. "Of the horrors perpetrated during those two days of *tête-à-tête* it is better to say nothing," writes Marcel Aymé, tongue in cheek.

In the meantime, all her sisters experience equal degradation, and some reform; some become worse than they were.

In the end, Sabina and Théorème rediscover each other, but are caught by the gorilla man, who murders them, puts them in a gunny sack which he throws in the river, and then cuts his own throat.

At the same second that Louise Mégnin (Sabina) was strangled, her "sixty-some-odd thousand sisters also gave up their last breaths, with happy smiles, their hands at their throats."

A ridiculous story, but full of invention and even a cockeyed logic which justifies the genre.

Jorge Luis Borges, a fine writer whose unique and intellectual plots are influencing writers today, has his work defined by Robert Gorham Davis: "Like Poe, Borges admires concentrated ingenious short stories that achieve their effects very quickly and engage the intellect as well as the emotions. 'The Garden of Forking Paths' begins like a spy thriller by Graham Greene or Ian Fleming, and ends with a plot device typical of that tradition."

In this tale written in the first person, "Dr. Yu Tsun, former teacher of English at the Tsingtao *Hochschule,* casts unsuspected light" on a historic event. He, in reality a double agent, tells how for a time he evaded Captain Liddell Hart, who has found him out.

Escaping with the "secret that he alone knew"—the name of the site of the new British artillery park on the Ancre—he takes a train into the country, which leaves just before Captain Liddell Hart can get on.

"The train crept along gently amid ash trees. It slowed down and stopped, almost in the middle of a field. No one called the name of a station. 'Ashgrove?' I asked some children on the platform. 'Ashgrove,' they replied. I got out."

Finding this, Yu Tsun muses, "Not for nothing am I the great grandson of T'sui Pên. He was Governor of Yunan and gave up temporal power to write a novel with more characters than there are in the *Hung Lou Meng,* and to create a maze in which all men would lose themselves." Yu Tsun arrives at last "at a high, rusty gate," to hear Chinese music coming from a pavilion. A man carrying a lantern "shaped like a drum and colored like the moon, came and opened the gate, saying in Chinese:

" 'No doubt you want to see the garden?'

" 'The garden?'

" 'The garden of forking paths.'

"Something stirred in my memory and I said, with incomprehensible assurance:

" 'The garden of my ancestor, T'sui Pên.'

" 'Your ancestor? Your illustrious ancestor? Come in.' "

He enters, to be greeted by the Sinologist, Stephen Albert, "watching me with a smile on his face. His face was deeply lined and he had gray eyes and a gray beard. There was about him something of the priest and something of the sailor. Later, he told me he had been a missionary in Tientsin before he had aspired to be a Sinologist."

Yu Tsun relaxes, calculating that his pursuer, Captain Hart, cannot arrive in less than an hour, and the two men talk about his ancestor. "He gave up all the pleasures of oppression, justice, of a well-stocked bed, of banquets and even of erudition, and shut himself up in the Pavilion of the Limpid Sun for thirteen years," says Stephen Albert. He then reveals a tall, lacquered writing cabinet. "Here is the labyrinth. A symbolic labyrinth." It is the manuscript of a book, from which he then reads.

After this they discuss the meaning of "The Garden of Forking Paths," which Stephen Albert explains, shows how the author "believed in an infinite series of times, in a dizzily growing, ever spreading network of diverging, converging and parallel times. This web

of time—the strands of which approach one another, bifurcate, inter-
sect or ignore each other through the centuries—embraces *every*
possibility. We do not exist in most of them. In some you exist and
not I, while in others I do, and you do not, and in yet others both
of us exist. In this one, in which chance has favored me, you have
come to my gate. In another, you, crossing the garden, have found
me dead. In yet another, I say these very same words, but am an
error, a phantom." He then goes on to say, "And in one of them
I am your enemy."

At this point Captain Liddell Hart is seen coming up the garden
path. Albert turns his back and the narrator, Yu Tsun, who "had the
revolver ready," fires "with the utmost care."

And why did Yu Tsun commit this act so deliberately? So that the
English newspapers of the world would report he shouted at the end,
"Albert!" thus revealing to the Germans the "secret name of the city
to be attacked" by the British.

Basically a simple plot, with delightful variations and style.

In most plotting, the cautious writer will not have frozen an ending in his mind until he has reached a point of no return on his
typewriter. For if the incidents in which he has placed his characters
turn out precisely as planned, he is in all likelihood not holding
himself loose enough for his imagination to be freely at work. Successful plotting, in the final accounting, is a combination of the
subject found, the imagination at work, and the mind intelligently,
but loosely, in control. At the end, when you have taken your reader
to the final pages, have let him feel with you that this is the only
possible way he himself would have things happen, then you may
close your mind and imagination.

The last words can only be these: in plotting, reject everything
that is irrelevant, and leave no part of the puzzle out of place.

# 2

# CHARACTER AND DIALOGUE

A YOUNG MAN from Mississippi once called on William Faulkner
and asked him to read a novel he'd written.

"Do I have to?" asked Faulkner.

"Well, no," said the embarrassed young author. "But maybe you
could just give me some advice about writing. . . ."

Mr. Faulkner thought a moment.

"Well," he said, "if you are going to write, write about *human
nature.* That's the only thing that doesn't date."

Some time later, in accepting the Nobel Prize for Literature,
Faulkner said his aim had been "to create out of the materials of the
*human spirit* something which did not exist before." There perhaps,
between the two, we have the scope of good fiction: human nature
and the human spirit embodied in the characters an author creates.

It is significant that Dr. Irving Langmuir, yet another Nobel Prize
winner, in chemistry, said something quite different, which may help
to explain the differences between science and art today.

"Do not," he said in an interview, "waste your time thinking
about *people.* The only way to live happily is to care more for *things.*"

While it has never been suggested that William Faulkner, given
another turn of the head in youth, might have been a scientist, the
evidence is clear: Dr. Langmuir could never have been a writer.
Because people, the characters around us, *are* a writer's chief concern, and even with years of constant vigilance we can never know
enough of the particularities, the weaknesses and strengths, the errors and nobilities of the human race. For a writer this lifetime study
is his way of life, his way of loving, a means of understanding, and
the base of his vocation.

How we choose people for our fiction does not matter, nor is it
ever predictable. Characters come upon an author sometimes when

he is least aware. Something about a stranger will hold our attention and remain in our memories until brought back into the light by some unexpected recognition of similarities with another; rarely is a fiction person drawn from one model only. We are seldom percipient or intuitive enough to know all about anyone without the underpinning of other examples—a man from our childhood, a contemporary of our late adolescence, a friend in our maturity. We recall other individuals a character reminds us of, or two or three observed in other circumstances, other states of mind, and if earlier we have had enough foresight, we will have recorded in a notebook the eccentricities of friend or stranger, and we will use these too.

E. M. Forster said that in no book did he put down "more than the people I like, the person I think I am, and the people who irritate me." And Chekhov wrote, "When men ask me how I know so much about men, they get a simple answer: everything I know about men, I've learned from me."

Aldous Huxley wrote that he tried to imagine how certain people would behave in certain circumstances. "To write fiction, one needs a whole series of inspirations about people in an actual environment and then a whole lot of hard work on the basis of those inspirations."

Frank Swinnerton, the octogenarian novelist, once wrote that he often thought about a group of imaginary characters and was "amused" by them to the point where he would begin to plan a story. Then: "I hear the voices of real people. . . . Sometimes I see a character going toward perdition," and he tries to stop him, without success. "*He* has chosen, and he can't go back."

If selection of dramatic events is the first task of an author, selection of traits of character must come next: where a rounded character does not exist in life, it is the writer's job to create him. This can be an unconscious process, sometimes only a vague feeling of understanding a person better than we have any reason to, sensing his potential for growth or trouble or mere weakness; again, sometimes it is a simple process of combining the traits of one or more individuals and seeing what comes out.

Any character of consequence must have, however, some root characteristics which easily identify him in a reader's mind. We needn't be told specifically that this man has a wart on his nose so we will remember who he is, or that he empties all his pockets every night before he goes to bed and fills them in the morning, in any direct way, but these things must be in the author's mind so that, if necessary, these identifying flaws, or habits, may be allowed to push through the action, giving a further sense of reality to the character, helping him come alive. Oliver LaFarge said we start out by "designing" our characters, but they are real only when we begin to create them—and, as with Swinnerton, when they take the final steps independently of their creator.

A very personal example in the creation of a fictional character was in my story "Cowboy and Child," in which one woman emerged from a stored memory of three actual, living individuals.

One real-life woman was dark, tense, and childless and treated her small dog as she would a child, preparing its food with the grim care of a nurse and seeing its ills as major catastrophes. Married to a silent, stolid man on whom she made little impression, she seemed forever on the verge of a breakdown, which never came.

Another woman, equally neurotic, with black, angry eyes, nervous hands and body, disliked all animals and hated dogs. She raised two children, without any outward show of affection, as well-mannered robots until her husband left her for another woman and the children ran away soon after.

A third woman, with similar coloring and physical characteristics, taller than the others, remained trapped at home with her aging, complaining mother and had a complete nervous breakdown when her mother died.

Somehow over the years these three women merged to become a single character in a short story about a woman named Marcia Gibson who arrives with her six-year-old daughter at a Reno ranch for a divorce. The cowboy in the title is Hank (who combined the traits of an actual cowboy and a New York publisher), manager of the ranch, riding master and lover of the ranch owner, Reba Smart. Late one night Hank meets the woman and child and drives them to the ranch.

"The little girl sat upright on her mother's lap and the cowboy could feel that the child's head darted and strained away from her body at every turn and at every sound in the night; her moments of quickness, like those of a young bird moving from cover to cover, were brief but startling and the cowboy found himself resenting the mother's indifference to the child, her lack of assurances against the night. . . . Hank knew this type of woman, had frequently been forced to accompany them in Reno, but he had not before seen such a woman with her young."

The mother further antagonizes Hank when the child begins following him about the ranch, and she accuses him of causing little Joan's nightmares. Soon thereafter, the father comes to Reno to see the child, and he speaks to Hank.

"I've been asking questions about you in town. . . . Thought I'd better—in view of what Mrs. Gibson says."

"Mmm." Hank feels the anger again tighten through his chest at the thought of the woman, but he does not commit himself.

"They say you're a pretty tough guy."

"I've killed a man or two."

Suddenly the man grins at Hank; he seems to want to make some further gesture when he says, "That's what I thought," and puts his hand on Hank's arm as though to show understanding. But his voice suddenly becomes without expression as he takes his hand away and asks, "Ever kill a woman?"

"Different ways of dealing with *them.*"

After the father leaves, the woman on his orders permits the child to ride with Hank until: "One morning, Marcia Gibson again came to the breakfast table dark-eyed and accusing and told them all somewhat shrilly that Joan had cried out in the night about the horses, and she was being driven to them and that she, Marcia, would take Joan to a doctor if Hank again interfered."

From here on the woman becomes increasingly irrational, until one day in a rainstorm she tears out to the stables, where the child has gone to see Hank. "Joan was humming to herself, and happy, patting a shiny brown colt."

The woman hysterically cries, "What have you been doing to her? Joan, baby, what has he *done* to you?"

Hank catches her by the arm as the child flees. She struggles, but then "sat down suddenly at his feet and looked up at him whimpering and rocking crazily. Then something else was there in her face, something evil to him, and shocking—yet sickeningly familiar."

Hank races away and gets in his car; and then he hears "a soft, frightened little sound" from the seat behind him. The child is there, and Hank "knew there was no choice, just as on a few other occasions in his life he had had no choice on what he knew he must do." He asks the child, "Do you want me to take you away, Joan? Do you want to go away from here with Hank?" She nods, and he goes back into the ranch for his pay from Reba Smart.

He is about to turn away when he hears the hired man calling from the barn. The child's mother has hanged herself.

In the end the father takes the child, and Hank is left with Reba; but it is the fictional mother, created from more than one neurotic woman met in passing, who dominates the story and arouses recognition in the reader's mind.

The other characters in this story can also be traced to remembered origins. Reba Smart, the cowboy's mistress, has in one form or another appeared in many of my works. Reba, a sensuous, experienced, practical but generally sympathetic character, was first a glamorous black-haired aunt I knew in childhood, a woman whose morals were questioned and gossiped about, but whose appeal to a romantic adolescent girl was unmistakable.

And the child? Perhaps the author herself had once been frightened by adult passions and responded to the kindness of a stranger.

Fiction writers must put themselves in their characters if their work is to have any value in interpreting and recording the state of man's mind and emotions; it is more necessary with some characters than with others. How else can we empathize, say, with a fourteen-year-old boy guilty of telling a lie, than by somehow seeing ourselves as a child faced with the same threat of punishment?

How can a woman write of an eighty-year-old grandmother without imagining how it must be, all those years from now, to see oneself in the dressing-table mirror which once reflected only youth and beauty? How was Tolstoi to understand the temptations of Anna Karenina to run off if he himself had not felt the impulse to go away forever?

Then there are those writers who write only about their own subjective feelings, their own particular and perhaps painful experiences, and the effect of everyone and everything on themselves. These writers can, of course, be among the great. Because they are never aware of the problems and distracting obligations of other men, they are free to perpetually examine, assess, and record their own emotional responses, their most intimate thoughts and visions. O'Neill, Proust, Genêt, Henry Miller—these and others made whole worlds of their tensely involved selves, although lesser writers have tried to do the same and have bored us by their conceits.

The great ones: it is not perhaps that these writers feel nothing for the rest of mankind, but rather that the forces within them contain so much turbulence and conflict and drama that there are not enough hours in a lifetime to put all this in order, to follow each new clue which develops as they burrow deeper and deeper, and try to find the secrets of the universe in themselves.

Sherwood Anderson wrote: "I guess what I think is that if you start to write of your own life experience you will find yourself more and more as you go along with it, stopping to think about this or that situation you have been in." But then he added, "This is pretty likely to get you to thinking more and more of others involved with you in the damned difficult business of living, this all the time leading you more and more out of yourself and into others."

Once we have chosen our characters, or they have chosen us, our task is to present these men and women, these individuals, to the reader with as little mechanical fuss and strain as possible. We must show what they feel, know what they think, see what they do, hear what they say, and be able to identify them by their names or characteristics as actual persons who will carry our narrative along. We must also know their backgrounds and be able to imagine them at some crucial instances of their lives.

A character not clear in a writer's mind cannot be understandable in the reader's. We must live with our characters for a while, hold imaginary conversations with them, insult them, love them, move among their friends and enemies. Forster said that a character in a book becomes real only when the novelist knows everything about him, and Trollope demanded that "on the last day of every month a character must be that much older." Emma Bovary was a real character whose life story fascinated Flaubert.

Every character should come to life early; rather, we must establish his importance the moment he appears on the scene. Chekhov's rule was that minor characters must be instantly identified and described, but that a major character can develop more slowly, so long as one makes sure the reader *is aware* how important he is to be. No gesture is too small, no characteristic is too minor for us to consider *insignificant*.

We may also repeat characteristics of one character as seen through the eyes of another, realize the importance of one character as he appears to others. But clearly, clearly. Each word of anticipation must be weighted with significance, so that there is no confusion over who is the observer and who is the chief actor.

For example, three men are waiting for a girl they have each known at various times, one intimately, the others superficially.

One asks, "Is Pam always late as this? At nineteen, I suppose she can't be bothered too much by time. I thought the first time I saw her—about six months ago, at the beach—that she had an unreliable look about her, but that may have been because of all that curly blond hair."

"She's not really unreliable, I shouldn't think. But concentrated in whatever she's doing or where she is, you know. When she's with you she gives you her whole attention. At least I thought so last fall when I took her to a football game."

The third man, who has been the girl's lover, says wisely: "Oh, I think she knows what she's about. I'm not sure that's what she wants us to think, though."

So what do we know about the girl in a few short paragraphs? Her name is Pam, she's nineteen, with curly blond hair, which gives her a flighty look that is perhaps deceptive. She's really a girl who likes men, although she's not as innocent about this as she would appear to be on a month's acquaintance. And she's not yet on the scene.

She is also a girl who has gone to football games enough to know what they are about. And she's clever enough to keep at least two men guessing; the third man is either jealous or disenchanted. We do not yet know what the girl thinks of him.

Perhaps we would go from here to Pam, coming in by plane. We could, with the license of the author, then reveal what she thinks of each of the men, and what she intends to do to put each one in his place, or to keep each one infatuated with her. Perhaps she understands she was too free with the last man on short acquaintance, and intends to use the others to show him how indifferent she can be. She may even be in love with this man, which gives us another view of her personality; and perhaps she has her hair now smooth and sleek, and can no longer be described as a curly blond. Finally, she herself will give us a clearer understanding of each man as *she* sees *him*.

Characters must have *sex, names, faces, speech,* which no author completely invents. He may combine a name out of a telephone book with the face of a great-aunt Mathilda, but only the combination will be new, not the characteristics.

*Sex* is determined the instant we have a story to tell. Sex lives, sex habits, sex needs are something else and must be treated in context with the characters. It is the gender, the decision whether we are to write about male or female, that is the important thing in the beginning.

*Names* must be chosen carefully and sometimes changed in the course of writing if a name does not seem to suit the character as he develops. Mary O'Hara notes in her exceptional book *The Making of a Novel* that it is hard to think about people, and impossible to talk about them, before they have names. "I work at their names awake and asleep, driving, resting, eating, visiting. For days or weeks I would struggle with one single character rightly to name him, actually a sort of mad seizure, shaking him by the throat—'Tell me! Tell me! What is your name? Your real name?'"

"For me, at least," she goes on, "the naming—right naming—is part of the very structure of the character. With the wrong name, the character looks wrong, talks wrong, does the wrong things."

Choose names that sound real but are not, understanding with the deepest intuition that names are an integral part of each individual, and that the wrong one can interfere with the creative process of delineating character.

Saul Bellow was once asked about getting "so right a name as Augie March" for his novel of that name. He had no explanation except that it just came to him as part of the general ease with which he wrote his book. "The great pleasure of the book was that it came so easily. All I had to do was be there with buckets to catch it."

Watch for subconscious association of names. Sometimes one finds he has inadvertently chosen one too close to a real-life character. Take, for instance, a name like Marvin Smyte, which no intelligent author would ever choose. But somehow, in our book, we have named the character based on him Marvin Tight, an equally unlikely name, and unfortunately it feels inspired, until the book appears in print. Then there is nothing we can do about it other than hope the real man will not sue us for libel.

Horatio Alger, Jr., said that "by request" he had "often given characters the real names of friends and acquaintances, without necessarily making them portraits." And he wrote in the *Ladies' Home Journal* in 1890, "I have always preferred to introduce real boys into my stories when it has been possible for me to find a character suited to a plot."

*Names* must evoke real persons. John Burnett, in his first novel, has a major character named Jason—idealistic, good-looking, and prepared to fight for what he wanted. The character became so real to the author, embodying most of the qualities he thought best in this generation's younger men, that he named his own son after the character in his book.

There are some simple rules. Have no two surnames with the same letter or sound, in order to avoid confusion between characters. Do not give short names of any similarity to two persons the reader may have trouble identifying at the start—*Henry,* for instance, and *Harry* could easily become confused in a reader's mind.

Actually, a telephone book, that standby of pulp writers, is as good as any source for names, particularly those of foreign origin.

If you give a girl a man's name, such as Tracey or Claude, make sure the sex is established at once; and if one idiosyncrasy can identify a particular character and no other, make this a part of your introduction of the man or woman at first sight.

*Faces* were always particularly described by the older novelists. We are frequently careless about this today, as though it does not matter. We say a character is blond or swarthy, short or tall. The rich descriptive language that actually evoked a complete and particular human being is too often ignored.

In *Crime and Punishment* Dostoevski wrote of Katerina Ivanovna: "She was a terribly gaunt woman, slender and quite tall and graceful; her hair was still a beautiful light brown and her cheeks were indeed flushed, with two red spots on them. She was walking backward and forward about her small room, her hands pressed to her bosom, her lips parched, and she was breathing unevenly and jerkily. Her eyes gleamed feverishly, but her gaze was sharp and still, and the impression of sickness was produced by the last light from the guttering candle end playing on this consumptive and agitated face. She seemed to Raskolnikov to be about thirty, and truly she was no mate for Marmeladov."

In contrast, "The Breadman" by Mary Heath (from the *Virginia Quarterly Review* and included in *The Best American Short Stories*) starts with a visualized character—to a point:

". . . Eileen came down to the kitchen in one of the negligees that had been part of her own trousseau a year ago this month: peach with spidery white lace around the neck and wrists, ill-fated, for the marriage had barely lasted out the honeymoon.

" 'Sweetheart, I haven't even made coffee yet,' said Mrs. Sprout. 'That was a good buy, you know. Half price, but it washed up like new. You have a real eye for a bargain.' It was the negligee she spoke of.

"Eileen held out the wide hem and dipped it back and forth. Mother and daughter studied its peachy mothy glamour. 'Shame I never really got my money's worth out of it,' and they both laughed gaily." But observe: even though Eileen is a major character—the daughter of the bride—in the story, this is all the description we ever have of her. Perhaps, by today's impatience, it is enough. But—

"When you pass a grocer sitting in his doorway," Flaubert told Maupassant, "or a concierge smoking his pipe, or a cabstand, show me that grocer and that concierge, the way they are sitting or standing, their entire physical appearance, making it by the skillfulness of your portrayal embody all their moral nature as well, so that I cannot confuse them with any other grocer or any other concierge; and make me see, by means of a single word, wherein one cab horse does *not* resemble the fifty others ahead of it or behind it."

Mary O'Hara says, again, that she has been "wondering about faces. . . . Is it really necessary to paint them vividly and in detail in a novel? Writers differ about this . . . some do and some don't. I must confess that when an author does not, I, the reader, do it for him . . . must absolutely have a definite picture . . . then find it upsetting to read on page fifteen that she is black-haired when I've been picturing a blond . . . should I then have allowed her to go faceless all these pages?"

Whit's strong belief was that the faces we recall in our fiction, bring into our work, are those we must, at one time or another, have "looked at intently, even with affection. That affection itself is a form of concentrated attention; and so is dislike marked often by this directed attention. The faces we can't place when we meet a second time," he believed, are "those we looked at with indifference and which left no impression; they could never be part of the characters in our writing."

Sherwood Anderson wrote in his journal: "There is the street of houses in which I sit with friends, that woman over there at a nearby table in a restaurant. . . . What is the meaning of that frightened look that flits over the face of that woman? . . . There is a man gesticulating and talking to himself as he walks along. What is troubling him? The little human meetings of people in the streets. . . ." The faces of the "little human meetings of people" marked some of the most poignant passages in Anderson's work and influenced more writers of his generation than any other—Hemingway, in particular, and all the others who were taught by Anderson's fiction to really see the faces they looked upon.

*Speech and dialogue.* Every individual with a personality of his own has his own manner of speech—rhythm, inflection, accent, emphasis, tone, the shaping of his sentences. Some speak rapidly, in broken sentences; some more slowly and correctly. We not only show the degree of education in a speaker's voice, but also his temperament, his feelings, his idiosyncrasies. Many writers, such as Chaucer, wrote primarily for the ear. It is said he *heard,* as he wrote, every line spoken by his characters.

We must catch the word patterns, knowing, as someone has said, that "a chance word out of place can reveal character as clearly as proof in a court of law that a man has committed murder." All dialogue should be of vital significance to someone.

John O'Hara claimed he'd inherited his ear for convincing dialogue from his mother, who had a gift of mimicry, and here again the arts of theater and prose writing are related. The words of dialogue must be read as though spoken; and the safest way for a writer to achieve this sense of familiarity is to speak his own words aloud, either in the process of writing, or in rewriting. Especially in rewriting, when we challenge dialogue to sound like the essence of the personality about which we write. Can it be heightened? Toned down? Expanded, deleted, rearranged, *cut out altogether? Speak* the words you have written, with varied inflections; practice, as Robert Frost advised, even your "Oh."

Once a shy, small boy had a part in a school play in which his responsibility was to come in at the right moment with "Oh." The adults around him took this as a funny matter—until he was heard from his room at night, when he thought no one was listening, speaking his "Oh" in every possible inflection. "Oh?" "Oh!" *"Oh."*

Watch the patterns of words; also remember that any dialogue has the obligation to advance the story action. Every word spoken must mean something to someone, and if a character says the day is hot, it must mean (a) that he is speaking of a triviality to conceal something we know he really means; or (b) that since the day is hot, something planned in this tale cannot take place, or if it does the weather will affect that event; or (c) that he is a complaining man and somehow blaming someone else for the weather.

Dialogue shows moods, changes in mood; it can reveal emotion, more by what is not said than by what is. We must not speak rhetorically in dialogue.

Speech must be within the education and culture of the speaker: we do not write intellectually over the head of a bus driver, or put profanity in the sermon of a Billy Graham.

Do not forget, as Galsworthy has said, and as Caldwell and Tennessee Williams and others have demonstrated in their work, the importance of a skilled use of humor. Galsworthy thought if one had to "give the palm to a single facet in the creation of character, it would be sly, dry humor." And any social discourse is made palatable in most dialogue with the inserted wit or lightness or contrasts we practice, nearly all of us, in our daily lives.

*Dress, dwellings, nationality,* all these too have a place in the creation of individuals the reader will care about and remember. It has been suggested that dull characters become more interesting against exotic backgrounds, that complicated and alien individuals stand out best against simplicity. But do not permit the life of any character to move without event for long in the course of your fiction: even if life is sometimes like this, it is not what the reader wants to remember.

In the end, once we have taken our characters through emotions, actions, happenings, and perhaps catastrophes, we must not fail to leave a reader with the conviction that all this is inherent in our character's makeup, part of his inevitable fate. Logic must guide us unmistakably to the end by means of reasonable reactions.

Finally, examine all characters for clichés in speech or action; for falseness; for woodenness and inconsistencies. Do not load on explicit emotions to make certain he will be understood, and do not permit your own feelings or prejudices or sympathy or dislike for a character to carry you into melodrama.

Our final hope for any character is that our reader has been so absorbed and convinced of what we have revealed and made significant, that in the end his own conclusions will be equal to our own. Joyce Cary has said that we sympathize with characters who have been in a jam, because all of us "are in a jam, a special and incurable difficulty from which there is no escape. It continues all our lives and affects every aspect of our existence." And so we conspire with our characters, as with our lives, to find solutions, to find release from tensions, to work them (and ourselves) out of the jam so that in the end we can believe it all means something after all.

Whit concluded that if our characters and our readers arrive at a point of revelation, new insight, or dissolving problems at the same time, convinced by our character's actions and propelled by convincing events toward a unified end, we have succeeded in our fiction, because then "we are in the other fellow's shoes."

# 3

# STYLE: THE MANNER
# OF THE TELLING

> Writing, to be effective, must follow closely the thoughts of the
> writer, but not necessarily in the order in which these thoughts occur.
> —E. B. WHITE, *The Elements of Style*

"MRS. HATTON BELIEVED that thought came first and one developed a writing style through much practice of putting his thoughts
on paper," wrote Jesse Stuart about his teacher in the Greenup
(Kentucky) High School, who first stimulated his desire to write.
"When I stop long enough to look back over the past, I think she
was one of the greatest English teachers that ever lived." And he
added conclusively that above all she warned, "One shouldn't just
try to do a style for style's sake."

He could never explain, Jesse said, how "gray-haired Mrs. Hatton, who never wrote a short story, essay, poem, or novel, who
never made a speech in public, who just taught school all her life and
kept a home for her husband and son, knew all these things about
creative writing." But with all of Jesse's achievements, his style,
which Samuel Butler might have been describing when he ad-
vocated just "common, simple straightforwardness," has remained
purely and singularly his own.

Many writers have had their say on style, and most of these state-
ments have some value. There is a truism that the best style is the
least noticeable, "the manner of which least stands in the way of the
matter presented." No one denies the strong influence that Hemingway's simple, direct style has had on American writers living today.

Faulkner, on the other hand, whose Sartoris and Compson families
of Jefferson, Mississippi, are known equally well in the literature of
the world, seemed to favor a more complex, evocative prose.

Faulkner was of the old South; Hemingway was of the North and the Middle West. Faulkner wrote in the tradition of Joyce, erecting Gothic cathedrals beside the simplicity of Hemingway's identifiable modern structures, in the manner of Anderson and Flaubert. Each went through a war, and while it was to some extent the same war, each wrote differently of his experiences. Both were Americans of the same generation; each was foremost in his fictional authority and perceptions, and each finally was appreciated by the great world beyond our shores, considered equally representative of the American culture. And yet consider their styles.

Consider William Faulkner in "A Rose for Emily," which has, as Ray B. West described it, "a general tone of mystery, foreboding, and decay."

Miss Emily Grierson, who has been a concern of the town for many years, living alone with only a Negro manservant and discouraging all others from entering her house, has died. During her lifetime these things have happened (told almost in conversational flashbacks):

Her father died and she refused to have him buried for three days, saying he was not dead. "Just as they were about to resort to law and force, she broke down, and they buried her father quickly."

"That was when people had begun to feel really sorry for her. People in our town, remembering how old Lady Wyatt, her great-aunt, had gone completely crazy at last, believed that the Griersons held themselves a little too high for what they really were. None of the young men were quite good enough for Miss Emily and such. We had long thought of them as a tableau: Miss Emily a slender figure in white in the background, her father a spraddled silhouette in the foreground, his back to her and clutching a horsewhip, the two of them framed by the back-flung front door. So when she got to be thirty and was still single, we were not pleased exactly, but vindicated; even with insanity in the family she wouldn't have turned down all of her chances if they had really materialized."

But then, after she was ill for a time, she took in a man to live with her, Homer Barron, a Yankee—"a big, dark, ready man, with a big voice and eyes lighter than his face."

Eventually he disappeared, and the people thought he had left her. But when she died, and the townsmen pounded down a door that seemed never to have been opened, they found the body of Homer Barron "apparently once lain in an embrace" on the bed.

Ernest Hemingway in giving Whit permission to reprint "The Short Happy Life of Francis Macomber" in *This Is My Best,* told him to say that "Mr. Hemingway thought that was as reprintable as any other of his stories." There is the Hemingway style, even in a routine permission.

This story is so well known that it is only necessary to remind a reader that it is about Francis Macomber and his wife, Margaret, on safari with Robert Wilson, a white hunter and guide. As the story opens Macomber has been carried into his tent in triumph, having killed his first lion. But it soon develops from the scornful attitude of his wife, and Macomber's own embarrassment, that he has actually bolted and that even the native gunbearers are aware of it, that it is Wilson who has shot the lion.

There seems only one way for Macomber to redeem his cowardice, and that is to kill an animal for himself. He knows his wife will probably leave him anyway, and that the night of his cowardice she has gone to Wilson's bed; but he makes a decision to hunt the buffalo.

They set out on the hunt and suddenly come across three old bull elephants, "three huge, black animals looking almost cylindrical in their long heaviness, like big black tank cars, moving at a gallop across the far edge of the open prairie. They moved at a stiff-necked, stiff-bodied gallop and he could see the up-swept wide black horns on their heads as they galloped heads out; the heads not moving."

Both men shoot; Macomber kills the first bull, Wilson the second; the third has gone into the bush. But Macomber has a great feeling of elation. "I feel absolutely different," he says.

They go in the bush after the third elephant, when suddenly they see him "coming out of the bush sideways, fast as a crab, and the bull coming, nose out, mouth tight closed, blood dripping, massive head straight out, coming in a charge, his little pig eyes bloodshot as he looked at them."

Wilson shot for the nose, "shooting too high each time and hitting the heavy horns, splintering and chipping them like hitting a slate roof," and then Mrs. Macomber in the car shot at the buffalo "with the 6.5 Mannlicher as it seemed about to gore Macomber and had hit her husband about two inches up and a little to one side of the base of his skull."

The dialogue at the end is in a style characteristically Hemingway's.

" 'That was a pretty thing to do,' he [Wilson] said in a toneless voice. 'He *would* have left you, too.'

" 'Stop it,' she said.

" 'Of course it's an accident,' he said. 'I know that.'

" 'Stop it,' she said.

" 'Don't worry,' he said. 'There will be a certain amount of unpleasantness but I will have some photographs taken that will be very useful at the inquest. There's the testimony of the gunbearers and the driver too. You're perfectly all right.'

" 'Stop it,' she said.

" 'There's a hell of a lot to be done,' he said. 'And I'll have to send a truck off to the lake to wireless for a plane to take the three of us into Nairobi. Why didn't you poison him? That's the way they do in England.'

" 'Stop it. Stop it. Stop it,' the woman cried.

"Wilson looked at her with his flat blue eyes.

" 'I'm through now,' he said. 'I was a little angry. I'd begun to like your husband.'

" 'Oh, please stop it,' she said. 'Please, please stop it.'

" 'That's better,' Wilson said. 'Please is much better. Now I'll stop.' ''

When fiction stresses less what is happening than to whom, or why, more subtleties may be brought into play. Samuel Butler was a straightforward fellow; Marcel Proust was not. Young Pontifex walks as straight a line as Butler's time and explanatory style allowed. Hemingway and Faulkner try to use it all, the facts, the characters, the subtleties, in a style peculiarly of their generation.

Sherwood Anderson's style was described by Waldo Frank. In spite of "occasional superficial carelessnesses of language," he wrote, "on the whole the prose is perfect in its selective economy and in its melodious flow; the choice of details is stripped, strong, sure; the movement is an unswerving musical fulfillment of the already stated theme. Like Schubert, and like the Old Testament story tellers, the author of *Winesburg* comes at the end of a psychological process; is a man with an inherited culture and a deeply assimilated skill."

In "I Want to Know Why" Anderson writes about a boy at the Saratoga races, a boy who loves horses and idealizes the trainer, Jerry Tilford.

"I liked him that afternoon even more than I ever liked my own father. I almost forgot the horses, thinking that way about him. It was because of what I had seen in his eyes as he stood in the paddocks beside Sunstreak before the race started. . . ."

The race is won, and the boy follows Jerry with some other men who are celebrating the race in a farmhouse "for bad women to stay in." He watches Jerry through the window, hears him bragging "like a fool. I never heard such silly talk." And then he sees him kiss a woman, "the one that was lean and hard-mouthed and looked a little like the gelding Middlestride, but not clean like him, and his eyes began to shine just as they did when he looked at me and at Sunstreak in the paddocks at the track in the afternoon."

The boy runs home and doesn't tell anyone what he's seen. But "I been thinking about it ever since. I can't make it out. Spring has come again and I'm nearly sixteen and go to the tracks mornings same as always, and I see Sunstreak and Middlestride and a new colt named Strident I'll bet will lay them all out, but no one thinks so but me and two or three niggers.

"But things are different. . . . What did he do it for? I want to know why."

Philip Roth, one of today's best writers but an erratically challenging stylist not only in his prose but also in his subject matter, writes appreciatively of his friend Saul Bellow's style. It "combines a literary complexity with a conversational ease, a language that joins the idiom of the academy with the idiom of the streets (not all streets —certain streets); the style is special, private, and energetic, and though occasionally unwieldy and indulgent, it generally, I believe, serves the narrative and serves it brilliantly."

Take this passage from *Herzog,* with Herzog remembering his second wife, who has left him. One day, in a Catholic church:

"She pushed the swinging door open with her shoulder. She put her hands in the font and crossed herself, as if she'd been doing it all her life. She'd learned that in the movies, probably. But the look of terrible eagerness and twisted perplexity and appeal on her face —where did that come from? Madeleine in her gray suit with the squirrel collar, her large hat, hurried forward on high heels. He followed slowly, holding his salt-and-pepper topcoat at the neck as he took off his hat. Madeleine's body seemed gathered upward in the breast and shoulders, and her face was red with excitement. Her hair was pulled back severely under the hat but escaped in wisps to form sidelocks. The church was a new building—small, cold, dark, the varnish shining hard on the oak pews, and balots of flame standing motionless near the altar. Madeleine genuflected in the aisle. Only it was more than genuflection. She sank, she cast herself down, she wanted to spread herself on the floor and press her heart to the boards—he recognized that. Shading his face on both sides, like a horse in blinkers, he sat in the pew. What was he doing here? He was a husband, a father. He was married, he was a Jew. Why was he in a church?"

The London *Times* once stated that Hemingway's style succeeded because of his artful way of using American vernacular, which they believed most characteristic of our writing. Robert Frost has written that there are really two kinds of language: "The spoken language and the written language—our everyday speech which we call the vernacular; and a more literary, sophisticated, artificial, elegant language that belongs to books. I myself could get along very well without the bookish language altogether."

"Writing, to be effective, must follow closely the thoughts of the writer, but not necessarily in the order in which these thoughts occur," wrote E. B. White in *The Elements of Style.* In other words, the arrangement of thoughts becomes the writer's vernacular.

A note by Whit Burnett: "Style has always been in my mind the author's Self, the creative expression of that Self." But, "If a writer becomes too vague, even though one enjoys the style of writing and manages to grasp the meaning somehow, intellectually I usually am left empty. Yet if you kill style for the sake of the story, on the other hand, you kill the 'I' of the author. Do we read the author or the story? I, for one, demand that each enhance the other. To be successful, the author's intentions must be both clear and implicit."

There are other styles in which greater subtlety prevails. Eudora Welty wrote of Willa Cather that the uniqueness of her style resulted from her skill in not giving us "the landscape but her vision of it; we are looking at a work of art." It is the angle of that vision which distinguishes one writer's style from another's, that angle which is the writer's exclusive property.

For the developing writer who is not yet certain how his own style may develop, such examples may not explain much. For all writers, however, there is one starting point which cannot be passed over:

the use of language and its suitability. To be a master of language is to be a master chef: in the preparation of gourmet dishes no ingredient is rare in itself. The seasonings and flavor may come from many sources, but the results are dependent on the skill and imagination of the chef, if he is to produce a unique dish. Caviar and corned beef would never be combined to make a pudding.

A writer like Erskine Caldwell did not use the elegant language of a Proust to write his *Tobacco Raod;* nor would Proust have written in the ribald manner of Balzac's *Droll Tales.* And it is hard to imagine J. D. Salinger creating *Franny and Zooey* in the style of Thomas Mann's *Mario the Magician.* Style is the product of a writer's culture, the imprint of his temperament, and his feeling for the requirements of the subject matter.

We also include here an example of a style which is having an influence on writers today. Donald Barthelme is described on the jacket of his book *City Life* as a "master of the languages used to conceal truth." Years after Eugene Jolas's *transition* magazine in Paris, far beyond Joyce or Kafka or Gertrude Stein, we read:

"Laughing aristocrats moved up and down the corridors of the city.

"Else, Jacques, Ramona and Charles drove out to the combined race track and art gallery. Ramona had a Heineken and everyone else had one too. The tables were crowded with laughing aristocrats. More laughing aristocrats arrived in their carriages drawn by dancing matched pairs. Some drifted in from Flushing and São Paulo. Management of the funded indebtedness was discussed; the Queen's behavior was discussed. All of the horses ran very well, and the pictures ran well too. The laughing aristocrats sucked on the heads of their gold-headed canes some more."

Style is, someone has wisely said, a matter of knowing when one has said enough.

We have metaphor and simile which may be used for visual and imaginative effect. These, however, must also be un-self-conscious, acting as instinctive amplification of our thought or imagery, and not used as an end in themselves. A writer of the stature of Elizabeth Bowen sometimes created metaphors that illumined whole passages; at other times she seemed to manufacture them as embellishments she felt obliged to insert.

A metaphor, to Virginia Woolf, was a means of "digging caves behind" her characters.

Use punctuation as it comes naturally, as an aid to breathing, or for emphasis in style, or rhythm, or emotion.

Paragraph also by instinct: one introduces a thought; one develops it; and one concludes its meaning. That's all there is to it.

Use shorter sentences for action; longer sentences for reflection or, sometimes, the development of an emotion with sensuous undertones. Anger is usually in staccato style.

Avoid colorless, tame, hesitant speech, and use active verbs when possible without strain.

# III
# A WRITER'S MATERIAL

# 1
# THE USABLE PAST

THE NOVELIST FRANK NORRIS once wrote that, given an impressionable child of eight, a good teacher could produce a writer ready with all the equipment he would need to create literature in his maturity. This presupposes that writing is no more than a trade to be learned, a trick to be revealed, an apprentice's hand to be guided. It does not allow for the accidents of growth and private discoveries, the bafflements and rewards of living and of loving, the challenges of the world we must eventually face alone. It does not consider the nature of man himself, and the usable past the writer is forever collecting. In general haphazard living we may miss out on some of the refinements of the art of writing, but it is in the accidental reaping of life that we find the ironies and dramatic qualities and paradoxes that give breadth and interest to works of art. And it is in contact with the outside world that we find human characters to represent such qualities.

Sainte-Beuve wrote of Molière that "he and his troupe peeked and probed into every corner of the old society, and held up to ridicule indiscriminately the conceit of the nobles, the inequality of matrimonial rights, the speciousness of religious hypocrisy." Molière's material covered "an immense territory which extended as far as the wall of the Church."

To train a child in observation of his own protected self has value if, in time, he decides to write his own life into a novel (which he will always do to some extent, in any case), perhaps creating a minor *Jean-Christophe* or *Portrait of the Artist as a Young Man;* but where would he go from there?

The history of publishing is cluttered with one-story, one-book authors who were able, with skillful technique, to produce art once from their preoccupation with the details of their own lives, but then never managed to write anything publishable again. Not being Romain Rollands or James Joyces, their material ceased to interest us.

Somerset Maugham says he asked himself from time to time if he would have been a better writer if he'd devoted his whole life to literature, leaving out his medical studies, his loves, and his amusements. The answer was unequivocally no, that it did not ever seem enough merely to write. He wanted also to make a "pattern of his life, not excluding all the other activities proper to man."

"Writing," Sherwood Anderson once wrote for *STORY,* in discussing the art of storytelling, does "concern, rather vitally, a man's outlook on life. It is all wrapped up in this outer thing . . . a man's relationships, his striving, if you will, for the good life." Anderson goes on to say, "In one's writing there should be inevitably, I think, a kind of new world opening out before your eyes."

We write from what we know, remember, see, hear, and sense from all that goes on around us, cultivating relentlessly the capacity to draw into ourselves every experience and emotion and memory that we can possibly make our own. Someone has said that it is the brain that actively grasps and operates on what is presented to it as sensation; the intellect is the instrument that adapts life to fiction. It is with the first that we develop the receptivity of the artist, but with the second that we find a use for what we have absorbed.

We begin this absorption process unconsciously from childhood, and we sometimes feel we must spill all we've stored away on an analyst's couch. This is sometimes a substitute for writing, although it may also be, one cautiously admits, a preparation for writing, within reason. Taking a small episode from childhood for which one was unjustly punished and which one has stored away for years with a sense of guilt, going back into the reasons, feelings, and meaning of it all, may relieve some of the pressures of living, and the same process of remembering and analyzing is also of value for the writer if it does not go too far. He will try to find a larger meaning in his own experiences, and this is the stuff writers use.

Most writers do go back into the usable past, sometimes at the beginning and sometimes later in their careers. In the beginning, creative remembering may stimulate the young writer by giving significance to half-forgotten episodes; later, rediscovering the past may bring back the original freshness of the creative impulse. Remembering our "disorders and early sorrows," as Thomas Mann so eloquently described the days of youth, may refertilize our gifts at a time when this is needed, and knowledge gained in later years may add depth and meaning to it all.

In *STORY,* we published many fine stories by authors emotionally and sensitively recording the past of their youth, William Saroyan's Western Union delivery boy, J. D. Salinger's troubled adolescents, John Knowles's prep school days in his "Turn with the Sun," the genesis of his novel *A Separate Peace,* perhaps the book best loved by college students in the 1960s—all these and others were by young writers just beginning to hold their own pasts in perspective.

On the other hand, "Sherrel" was written by Whit when he was not so young. And yet this story of remembered guilt so perfectly expresses the deeply troubled state of a nine-year-old boy, it has been reprinted hundreds of times in many languages.

The story, told by Martin, begins: "You see, I actually did have a brother. People sometimes ask me, are you the only boy in the family? And I've said Yes. This wasn't a lie wholly. I was the first born."

The story goes on to tell of Sherrel, Martin's five-year-old brother. "He was a beautiful child. This was the brother I killed."

Their family lived near the sand hills, and one day "a cloudburst drenched them, rolling down soft sand, cutting great ditches in the road in front of our place . . . gnawed with caves and dangers." The older boys were playing in a ditch when Sherrel climbed down beside them. Martin's hands were peeling in a mysterious way, and the other boys were examining them. Sherrel wanted to see too.

Martin became angry and pushed Sherrel back, talking and scolding, talking in his face. No one knew then that the peeling hands indicated a light case of scarlet fever, and that he was giving it to Sherrel.

When Sherrel died, Martin thought, "I gave him that sickness. I knew that. That killed him. That is why my brother is dead."

And he remembers, with a further sense of guilt, what he'd said when Sherrel was born. "I said, 'There's enough in this family already.'

"That is how I figure it now. I killed my brother by meanness. And it is too bad. I wouldn't do it now."

Martin begins to imagine how it would have been had Sherrel lived. How he could have said to him, "You've got good stuff in you, I can tell. You're going to be an artist. So am I. We'll be two artists, brothers, maybe different, but we can help each other. . . ."

The story is a classic pattern of childhood guilt, remembered as passionately by the mature writer as when it occurred to the child.

Peter De Vries's first story, "Eine Kleine Nacht," was a sharply sensual tale of a young love affair, in which Tommie is drawn into June's bed for too long a time.

"Suddenly, when it was too late, Tommie heard the sound of feet" —the girl's parents—" near the top of the stairs. Then the bedroom door went open, the awful light flashed on, then quickly off again. Their hearts vaulted to their throats and their insides seemed to stream out of them, leaving a stupid hollow of fear."

There is a scene with the parents, the beginning of a fight, and Tommie is told to leave. "I'll see you," he heard June call. "Yes," he said. Then he slammed the door.

"The cold and the snow stung his face with a delicious sharpness. He put his overcoat on. He put his handkerchief again to his mouth. It was pretty well soaked with blood. It had turned much colder. He drew his collar up. The cold was sweet and keen and so was the snow. He held his head up to feel the flakes flutter on his face and in his eyes. He reached down, scooped up a handful of the snow and wiped it on the corner of his mouth where the big cut was. He took another handful, then another. The cold of it smarted on his hot face and on his cut lip, but it felt good. He walked on, his face held up to the thick flakes, feeling the wind and the cold, and once in a while he stooped down for a handful of snow to rub on his mouth from which blood still trickled." And there the story ended, a bittersweet re-creation of an early love.

"The cold was sweet and keen and so was the snow. . . ."

Carson McCullers was eighteen when "Wunderkind" appeared in *STORY.* She says of it, " 'Wunderkind' was the first short story I ever published and I was seventeen or eighteen years old at that time. I was very much thrilled to be in *STORY* Magazine and I bought lots of chocolate cake with the $25 they paid me."

"Wunderkind" is a tale about the tragic discovery of a fifteen-year-old child prodigy, a *wunderkind,* that she no longer has either the feeling for the piano or the talent for the music she has loved.

At her lesson with Mr. Bilderbach, she had been at the piano for almost three hours and was very tired. "His deep voice sounded as though it had been straying inside her for a long time. She wanted to reach out and touch his muscle-flexed finger that pointed out the phrases, wanted to feel the gleaming gold band and the strong hairy back of his hand."

But the lesson is a failure, even when Mr. Bilderbach worriedly tells her to go back to the first piece she'd ever studied with him, "The Harmonious Blacksmith." "I know you so well," he says, "as if you were my own girl. I know what you have—I've heard you play so many things beautifully. You used to—"

And then it is over. "Dragging her books and satchel she stumbled down the stone steps, turned in the wrong direction, and hurried down the street that had become confused with noise and bicycles and the games of other children." So it ends.

Carson's own life had been spent on music from the age of six, but her training was halted by a period of illness when she was fifteen. It was then she began to write short stories, and this story, written in Whit's class at Columbia, is obviously autobiographical.

*Where do we find our material?* Whit believed that at certain periods in life the writer must take time out to *saturate himself in his world.* To store our ideas, happenings, and tragedies as catalysts to stimulate the writing need within us. To be so filled with the demands, pleasures, extravagances, and paradoxes of life and our society that when the time for writing comes upon us, focus may be made swiftly and naturally from the selection of events and characters already assembled in our mind.

"Possible stories, presentable figures, rise from the thick jungle as the observer moves, fluttering up like startled game, and before he knows it indeed he has fairly to guard himself against the rush of importunate wings." Whether this was Whit's own unique way of putting it, or quoted from something he'd read, I do not know; but it was what he believed, and it represented his own conclusions.

Places have color, mood, significance in memory, and threat or promise. The New England farm in *Ethan Frome* and the landscape of cold isolation were essential for the tragic implications of the plot.

Lawrence Durrell has made Greece an exciting world interpreted by an Irishman and influencing writers of many languages. D. H. Lawrence never ceased his search for new environments and places in which to establish his own sensory, philosophical, sexual view of life and men and women. Paris of the 1920s haunts all those who came after, a Shangri-la for artists and writers who may or may not have reached the summit. Joyce, Galsworthy, Faulkner, Hawthorne, each had his *place* established, and whether their characters and fictional events came before or after the place, there is no separation between them. Literal or not, a house from one part of the world may be erected on ground in another; a sunset experienced over a windmill in Holland may carry that windmill to a Maine farm.

While the world of the author can no longer be a brand-new India, as it was with Kipling and E. M. Forster, or the Paris of Fitzgerald and the Pamplona of Hemingway, each author has some world of his own as his possession, to draw upon with all its scenes and the people in it. As an author, it is you who will decide what you then want to do with the world you feel is uniquely your own.

Your material is of course primarily the characters you have known, not only as you have experienced them, or see them now, but as they may have been in their own private pasts. Ask yourself about a woman who has interested you. What was she like as a child? Is she competitive with a man, or too submissive, too soft and eager to please? Is she vain? Has she good health, and what does she know or like about food? Is she capable of growth, understanding, tenderness—or is there an inner rigidity or frigidity which will defeat and undermine all her relationships? What does she want, or possess, or do? If she is already defeated, what in particular, or which moments in her life have defeated her? Put this character, and others, in an environment, or place, and see how one reacts upon the other.

Once, in a class, students were asked to write down any useful suggestions for finding material, for the stimulus to get started on a story, or a novel.

"Meet somebody new. Then my imagination starts to work. He says something and I turn it over in my mind. Maybe it worries me. I keep thinking about this and about him. Then in order to get it off my chest, I must write about him, and then forget it. Forget him."

"An observed character or episode stirs me quickly and forcibly, and that becomes the nucleus of a story. Sometimes it starts as no more than a half-formed fancy, which hopefully will grow."

"I sit down with all my tools and try to collect impressions of interesting people. All my life I have been adding to that subconscious repository."

"I find difficulty getting original ideas, but we all have a lot of unused material in our subconscious minds, I think. Accidental things suggested by conversation with someone, or a passing face— or even a newspaper paragraph, or some memory of an experience abroad. If I can remember, *start* remembering, things happen."

"I sit down at my typewriter and hope for the best."

It was Chekhov, who said as a final resort: "If you look long enough at anything, say just that wall in front of you—it will come out of that wall."

Shakespeare said, "And as imagination bodies forth the forms of things unknown, the poet's pen turns them to shapes, and gives to airy nothings a local habitation and a name."

Almost any unresolved emotion may fertilize the writing impulse, lead us to a character or a subject with which we will embody these feelings. *Anger, jealousy,* and of course *love:* in the end, one finds that almost any emotion one has ever had comes out somehow in one's work, and so it should, provided we use such stimulation wisely and well. Joseph Blotner wrote that Faulkner's fiction grew out of "his total life experience," and perhaps it is necessary to feel much, before one's writing will carry true conviction.

*Anger* may be a particularly fertilizing force on the writer; perhaps it is the most common impetus of all, if we want to write with passion and conviction. Dostoevski was angry all his life, Theodore Dreiser and Sinclair Lewis and Faulkner and Steinbeck all raged frequently in their work and pointed out in their best fiction the affairs of life as corrupted and perverted and abused by those who passionately disturbed them. Injustice, war, one's own failing powers, deceit in high places, death—if one did not care about the tragedies of life, particularly as these are caused and imposed on, and by, man himself, perhaps one would not think of writing at all. *"J'accuse!"* wrote Emile Zola, and helped set France on fire.

When "Address Unknown" first appeared in *STORY* in 1938, it caused a literary sensation. Kressmann Taylor said she wrote this powerful story of the brutality and deviousness of the Nazi days in Germany "to investigate what happens to a man who embraces a destructive principle. To follow the way in which the glossing over of an evil intent hardens a man's spirit and leads to the injury of others."

The story, as some may recall, is a series of letters between Max, the Jewish half-owner of an art gallery in San Francisco, and his former American-German partner, Martin, a Gentile, who has moved back to Hitler's Berlin. During the course of their correspondence, Martin reveals his increasing admiration for Hitler and what he is accomplishing, and this is a cause for distress to Max, who still cannot believe it all is happening. Not until his young actress sister, Grisell, is jeered from the stage in Berlin as a Jewess and goes to Martin for help, which he refuses, does Max understand how deeply Martin has been corrupted. He has rejected the girl, fearing reprisals against his own family if he helps a Jewess; she is killed by a Nazi gang when he turns her away. It is then Max starts on his campaign of revenge.

He cables Martin at his German bank as though they were still the closest of friends and also conspirators, and follows this with letters in which he pretends they are doing some mysterious business— preparing paintings for an exhibit, which seems to be a blind. He knows these letters are read by Nazi authorities as though they were written in a code, and Martin writes back in panic asking Max to stop writing.

Max continues, and by return letters the reader learns that Martin loses his job, being suspected of crimes against the Nazi state; he is persecuted; and finally, Max's last letter is returned, stamped *Address Unknown.*

*Jealousy* is an emotion Gertrude Stein once complained was most neglected in fiction; but at the time she spoke, Colette was still alive and writing her brilliant and perceptive books on the various aspects of love, with jealousy often enough the force which provided the drama and the wisdom.

In "Duo," a story about a *ménage à trois,* a wife discovers that her husband's secretary is also his mistress. Her struggle against jealousy leads to her eventual acceptance of the situation and forms an entire philosophy of Colette's world and wit. Rarely by any writer have the lacerating effects of jealousy been more dramatically or convincingly explored.

*Love* is hard to find in fiction, and when a love story did come in to the magazine, we all rejoiced. Sex is so much easier to dramatize; disappointed love ending in tragedy makes drama; but a love story concerned with ordinary feelings and dependencies and the growth and tenderness of a good relationship between a man and a woman is perhaps too banal for most writers to tackle. As a result, the subject becomes even more trite in the hands of the Erich Segals, and surely it is the most neglected theme in quality writing of the day. Let beginning writers take note: try to write of *love* with originality and conviction and persuasion, and editors will be eager to publish your work.

Perhaps, finally, we have our concern with—as someone has said —the unsolvable problem of man against evil, and beyond that, man's relationship with God. Some of us will tackle these concerns, but few will solve them. Seán O'Faoláin said, "The framework of the artist's ideas is clearly only that which he is forever seeking for universality, and must be far wider than the framework of the ideals of the patriot."

And Pasternak wrote that the greatness of the writer has nothing to do with the subject matter, but has much to do with how the author is touched by the subject.

# 2

# READING

There is no doubt in my mind that the chief reason that so many of the great classics seem to speak so directly to us is that the authors were consciously trying to reach us, or at least people with an astonishing resemblance to us.

—MASON W. GROSS, National Book Committee, November 1959

A good style simply doesn't *form* unless you absorb half a dozen top-flight authors every year.

—F. SCOTT FITZGERALD, letter to his daughter

SUGGESTIONS FOR READING usually are placed in an appendix, a sort of afterthought one may take or leave. Everyone reads: all writers must have read thousands of books during their lifetimes, or they would not now be trying to arrange their own sentences and paragraphs and images on a page, hoping for someone to read them. Let's just take it for granted that writing comes from a love of books, an obsession with authors, and familiarity with what has been written before we were born, or at least before we started to write. Ideally, this is true. It should be one of the end products of all writing, done today or yesterday or tomorrow, to further refine our language, to add color and meaning and eloquence to ordinary words and phrases used by average men, to give new dimensions and make new combinations of words which will enlarge our vision and our understanding of life.

But what fiction do we read? How many fine new novels are overlooked for those that appear on the best-seller lists each week? Or even on library lists? This is not the place to argue that too many readers are drained away from books because the easy channels of television and news and such are always open. This is a time to plead that if a writer has not read sufficiently in the past, it's time to do so now. If you've never read many novels, even the great ones, don't try to write one until you do. And if you've never read any short stories of quality and depth, don't think you know what a short story is all about.

Once at *STORY* we faced a bitter fact. While our subscription lists kept narrowing down, and our newsstand sales were pitiful, our incoming manuscripts were increasing daily, and the quality was worse and worse. At one time we found that in a week's time we had read more dull stories by ambitious writers than the total number of subscribers to the magazine!

So we wrote a form letter to be included with each manuscript, those we bought and those we returned. "Dear Author," we began, and spelled out the whole sorry tale, how we were delighted to receive their manuscripts, but someone had to keep a magazine going and subscribers were one very small source of revenue, and wouldn't they consider *reading* and then subscribing to our magazine *before* they asked *us* to *read* their work? Apparently the writers didn't even read this, for the stories came in greater numbers, especially the poor ones, as long as we had a magazine.

Now it may be argued that some of these writers had done their reading earlier and now felt it was time to settle down at their typewriters and create their own fiction. This is a valid point. There are years for reading much, and years for writing much, and the time-for-reading years do seem generally to have ended when one is no longer very young. Henry Miller says that in the days before he started to write, reading was "at once the most voluptuous and the most pernicious of pastimes."

It is also valid to say that once one starts writing seriously, one has less time and less patience with the way another writer may express himself. Obsession with our own subject matter may help us reject their novels, and there are those hours of a day a writer must manage to keep for himself.

Yet it is hard to imagine that one who has never fallen in love with a book, anybody's book, can ever fall intelligently in love with his own. The writer whose mind and emotions have never been deeply concentrated·on the character in a novel, or on the events of a fictional individual's life, can never truly make us believe in a fictional character of his own creating.

We read when young for a variety of reasons: to be entertained with stories and adventures of characters larger than ourselves but not incompatible with what we imagine our possibilities to be. To learn something of the vast world outside before we have to face it, and to discover facts about human nature and our own. To learn more about love and about sex and all the subtleties and range of love and sexual relations; to bolster our faith in an orderly world; to imagine ourselves as the author, and this in time may be the impetus that leads to our own writing.

What leads us into reading is determined by many things and persons: a librarian, a parent, a teacher, our own discoveries. Consider the short story by Bernard Malamud, "A Summer's Reading."

George Stoyonovich was a boy who had quit high school on an impulse at sixteen, worn out the patience of his family, and was ashamed every time he went looking for a job when people asked him if he had finished school and he had to say no. He began staying in his room most of the time, and when he was asked by the neighbors what he did with himself he said he read a lot. He also walked a great deal.

One time on a walk he met Mr. Cattanzara, who worked in a change booth in an IRT subway station. When he asked George what he was doing this summer, George said, "I'm reading a lot to pick up my education."

Mr. Cattanzara, interested, asked George what he was reading. George said he had a list of books from the library, maybe around a hundred. He was going to read them that summer.

After this, when George saw the neighbors smiling at him he understood that Mr. Cattanzara had told them about his reading. Then he found that his father and sister had heard about it too and were proud of him. This went on for a time; but eventually Mr. Cattanzara faced him and asked: "Name me one book so I can ask you a question on it!" And George knew he was found out.

Soon thereafter his sister asked, "Where do you keep the books you read? I never see any in your room outside of a few cheap trashy ones."

Now George was disgraced and avoided everyone, staying in his room for a week. But when he did go out, he found that people didn't seem to know yet what a fake he was.

And it ends: one evening in the fall, George runs out of his house to the library, where he hasn't been in years. There are books all over the place, wherever he looks, and though "he was struggling to control an inward trembling he easily counted off a hundred, then sat down at a table to read."

And eventually, perhaps, to write.

All reading, absorbed and digested, can teach a writer something. Almost any kind of books into which he can transfer his own sense of awareness, abandon his guardedness and mistrust, may be what he needs to know someday as a writer. Shirley Ann Grau once said, "In brief, I spend half my time trying to learn the secrets of other writers—to apply them to the expression of my own thoughts."

It is by reading that we learn first to focus the fiction mind, framing incidents and characters and places into the particular shape of imagery and economy that makes a short story, a play, or a book. A photographer has his own way of shutting off what he does not wish to see, moving his camera through many angles until he finds the one that suits him best—but this is after he has learned the limits of his medium.

The fiction writer's eye is not so very different. We eliminate extraneous detail, focus on this or that plane of a face, that telltale curve of a sneering lip; or we highlight certain corners of a room, blanking out others. Even though we make our own designs in the end, by reading we learn that patterns imposed on experience are the framework of our fiction.

Each author worth his weight pulls his own load and goes his own way (to skip to another metaphor). But without being exposed to the fictional achievements of others, it is likely we would spend the rest of our lives writing with no more depth than that found in the morning newspaper.

We also learn technique from books we read, the use of dialogue, the description of a place. Certain writers, such as Chekhov and Hemingway, have taught us dialogue for all time; other writers have shown us how in one sentence we can change a pace, a mood, an idea so skillfully the reader hasn't seen what was happening, but knows he has somehow got from one point to another farther on. To sum it all up, we read for two reasons: to be instructed and to be entertained.

Literature, someone has said, has three dimensions: breadth, depth, and elevation. The breadth comes from our experience, but also our recognition of this experience shared with other writers. Depth, which is no more than understanding, is limited only by the searching mind and its energy; and how better to understand human nature than by the reading we have done? Elevation is the distance we travel with our subject matter—its meaning, its symbolism, the larger and wider view from which we may survey all that has been done before—and written, in Dostoevski's *Brothers Karamazov,* in D. H. Lawrence's *Women in Love,* in Thomas Mann's *Magic Mountain.*

To quote from an article by H. B. in *The Writer's Year Book:*

"If a work of art must be separated in its unique particularity from the world around it, one of the earliest things a writer must learn is to separate his thinking and his writing from the thinking and writing he might be practicing if he were not setting out to write a short story [or a novel]. That is, he must get himself into a fictional state of mind, to see things as fictional possibilities. One help is to read fiction. Eventually something you read may touch off something in your own experience as suddenly obviously usable material for a story of your own. Fiction grows, like love, by what it feeds on. The fiction mind is more than a recording mind, it is a recording mind with imagination, flair, taste, point of view, all brought into focus by a personality which can see and relish the human condition. Adolescents read to the point of intoxication. Indeed, it may be the only time in life when fiction may seem more real than reality. That, for a fiction writer, is a valuable state of mind. So read and read some more, so that your bloodstream is charged by the alcohol of fiction and you come, at last, to feel and see and believe in the visions that fill your head."

The following is a personal list, and undoubtedly should be supplemented by other writers. (By all means, reader, do so!)

As children, we must have read the following:

Stories by:

| Edgar Allan Poe | Aesop |
| The Brothers Grimm | Charles Dickens |

Also:

| *Swiss Family Robinson* | *My Friend Flicka* |
| *King Arthur and His Knights* | *Alice in Wonderland* |
| *Robinson Crusoe* | *Wind in the Willows* |
| *The Wizard of Oz* | *Huckleberry Finn* and |
| *Kipling's Jungle Book* | *Tom Sawyer* |

As adults we should have read some novels by the following:

Gustave Flaubert

Honoré de Balzac

Marcel Proust

Dostoevski

Leo Tolstoi

D. H. Lawrence

Henry James

F. Scott Fitzgerald

Virginia Woolf

Jane Austen

E. M. Forster

W. H. Hudson

James Joyce

Somerset Maugham

Solzhenitsyn

Franz Kafka

Ernest Hemingway

Thomas Mann

Isak Dinesen

Hermann Hesse

Sinclair Lewis

Saul Bellow

Thornton Wilder

William Faulkner

Laurence Sterne

Joseph Conrad

Arnold Bennett

Turgenev

Maxim Gorki

Aldous Huxley

Sinclair Lewis

Sigrid Undset

Stendhal

Emile Zola

Herman Melville

Thomas Wolfe

John Galsworthy

Thomas Hardy

Albert Camus

William Styron

Ivy Compton-Burnett

Norman Mailer

Mark Twain

Philip Roth

George Orwell

Vladimir Nabokov

Short stories by:

Anton Chekhov

D. H. Lawrence

Eudora Welty

Flannery O'Connor

Bernard Malamud

J. D. Salinger

Sherwood Anderson

Katherine Anne Porter

Katherine Mansfield

Erskine Caldwell

H. E. Bates

William Saroyan

Boccaccio

Frank O'Connor

Mary Lavin

Truman Capote

Edgar Allen Poe

Nathaniel Hawthorne

Whit Burnett

Novellas by:

Henry James

Alberto Moravia

Colette

Stephen Crane

|                    |                        |
|--------------------|------------------------|
| Edith Wharton      | Katherine Anne Porter  |
| D. H. Lawrence     | Kay Boyle              |

Other works by:

|                    |                        |
|--------------------|------------------------|
| Shakespeare        | George Santayana       |
| Sigmund Freud      | William James          |
| C. G. Jung         | Henry David Thoreau    |
| Aristotle          | Ignazio Silone         |
| Eugene O'Neill     | Chaucer                |
| Ibsen              | Henry Miller           |
| Luigi Pirandello   | Mary McCarthy          |

Also *This Is My Best,* by Whit Burnett—1942 and 1970.

Remember, Maupassant read Flaubert; Maugham read Maupassant; Katherine Mansfield read Chekhov; Chekhov and James read Turgenev; Hemingway read Sherwood Anderson and Gertrude Stein; Thomas Wolfe read everybody.

Elizabeth Nowell, in her excellent book on Wolfe, quotes from *Time and the River:* "to prowl the stacks of an enormous library at night, to tear the books out of a thousand shelves. . . . The thought of these vast stacks of books would drive him mad . . . the greater the number of books he read, the greater the immense uncountable number of those which he could never read would seem to be. Within a period of ten years he read at least 20,000 volumes . . . and opened the pages and looked through many times that number. . . . He pictured himself as tearing the entrails from a book as from a fowl. . . . Walking at night among the vast piled shelves of the library, he would read, watch in hand, muttering to himself in triumph or anger at the timing of each page: 'Fifty seconds to do that one. Damn you, we'll see!' . . . and he would tear through the next page in twenty seconds."

Perhaps it is true, as Henry Miller wrote, that in certain books "there are lines, just lines page so-and-so, top left, that stand out like mountain peaks—and they made you what you have become."

# 3
# NOTEBOOKS AND DIARIES

THERE IS LITTLE difference between keeping a notebook and a diary, for the writer. Granted, the diary is often confessional and private, and the notebook more often records the thoughts, aphorisms, and perhaps travel notes less subjectively observed. In the end the impulse is to put down feelings, opinions, the effects of other individuals on our lives or on the world around us. Virginia Woolf in her *Writer's Diary,* for example, tells only a little more about her personal life and the demands of her society than Henry James in his more obviously literary *Notebooks,* in which he also records names of guests at dinner parties, and the world of his time, while clearly developing his ideas for his stories and novels step by step.

Virginia Woolf wrote from Juan les Pins in May 1933: "Yes, I thought, I will make a note of that face—the face of the woman stitching a very thin, lustrous green silk at a table in a restaurant where we lunched at Vienne. She was like fate—a consummate mistress of all the arts of self-preservation: hair rolled and lustrous; eyes so nonchalant; nothing could startle her; there she sat stitching her green silk with people going and coming all the time; she not looking, yet knowing, fearing nothing; expecting nothing—a perfectly equipped middle-class Frenchwoman." Virginia Woolf was preparing for her work as much as Henry James in his *Notebooks.*

On a January Saturday in 1895 James wrote:

"Note here the ghost-story told me of Addington by the Archbishop of Canterbury: the mere vague faint sketch of it . . . of a lady who had no art of relation and no clearness; the story of the young children (indefinite number and no age) left to the care of servants in an old country house, then the death, presumably, of the parents. The servants, wicked and depraved, corrupt and deprave the children; the children are bad, full of evil to a sinister degree. The servants die (the story vague about the way of it) and their apparitions, figures, return to haunt the house and children, to whom they try to beckon, whom they invite and solicit from across dangerous places, the deep ditch by the fence, etc.—so that the children may destroy themselves, lose themselves, by responding, by getting them in their power. . . . It is all obscure and imperfect, the picture, the story, but there is a suggestion of strangely gruesome effect in it. The story to be told—tolerably obviously—by an outside spectator, observer."

Not until three years later, in 1888, did James write *The Turn of the Screw,* which appeared in a *Collier's Weekly* of that year. Remember James's incisive formula on how to create a sense of evil: "Make him [the reader] think the evil, make him think it for himself, and you are released from weak specifications."

A notebook or a diary need not be written in every day, although some pattern of recording is desirable.

Some write in notebooks only when they are away from home, traveling, recording new impressions for which ordinarily no hook of memory might be found. Some write only when they are not working. George Sand wrote in her journals when she was not in love; when she was "normal"—that is, "desperately in love"—she wrote her novels.

Others wait until the love affair is ended—"emotion remembered in tranquillity," as Wordsworth has said.

At certain periods in our lives we find ourselves more introspective, having recognizably literary thoughts and conclusions and no one to share them with; at other times we may simply record events, trusting to memory to bring back the whole of the picture (but memory does not always humor us).

The notebook, being private, permits us to draw no morals, obey no rules, censure no extravagances. We write for ourselves only and need show no one what we have written. Sometimes, years later, a notebook will be published to the benefit of other writers; sometimes, like my Aunt Margaret's diary, it will be kept for a lifetime, recording weather, events of the day, family events, and then at the end no one cares and the journal is thrown in the fire.

For the writer, first impressions are to be seized upon, and the act of writing in a journal often ensures that these impressions are permanently recorded. We write a quick paragraph about a character, and do not look at this again; but years later we may find we have written about her, described her, so we think, from some image in our mind—then find we have simply used from memory the description we recorded long ago.

Van Wyck Brooks has said that the "writer is important only by dint of the territory he colonizes," and this colonizing for a writer simply means that he has put down impressions and observations in words which are his own.

Self-criticism: "At forty," wrote Virginia Woolf in her diary, "I am beginning to learn the mechanism of my own brain—how to get the greatest amount of pleasure out of it. The secret: I think always so to continue that work is pleasant."

Observations of life: Coleridge in his notebooks observes the behavior of children, reports his dreams, and queries about natural phenomena, making as well philosophical and psychological speculations. He also records "recipes for beef stew, and details of an illness."

Chekhov, on the other hand, makes aphorisms:

"Women deprived of the company of men pine; men deprived of the company of women become stupid."

"A woman is fascinated not by art, but by the noise made by those who have to do with art" (sic!).

"N. has written a good play; no one praises him or is pleased. They all say: 'We'll see what he writes next.' "

"A man married to an actress, during a performance of a play in which his wife was acting, sat in a box with beaming face and from time to time got up and bowed to the audience."

How much Anton Chekhov actually used the notes in stories and plays is less easy to determine than with some writers, such as Arnold Bennett, who not only wrote out his plots in his journals, but frequently scolded himself for wasting his time. But it does not matter. We may not know how or if we shall use this notebook writing in our stories or novels, but making recording a habit will add another tool to our powers of expression, our uses of observation, and the total value of the material we accumulate.

Mark Twain, Katherine Mansfield, Stendhal (Henri Beyle), André Gide, Anthony Trollope—all these and many others have left behind some of their most piquant words in notebooks, journals, and diaries, and sometimes in letters, all of which show the writers' minds most intimately at work.

Better, of course, to write our own observations if we intend being writers; but to stimulate our thoughts and creative juices it helps to read these others, to feel a kinship with Virginia Woolf when she wrote: "December 28th, 1945. It's all very well to write that date in a nice clear hand, because it begins this new book."

A unique production was Dostoevski's *Diary of a Writer*, described by Pushkin as:

> His mind's dispassioned observations
> And doleful records of his heart.

In his published diary Dostoevski wrote down everything: the political situation, appreciation and criticism of other writers, reminiscences. Treasure such observations as:

"Take a Russian drunkard and compare him, let us say, with a German drunkard: the Russian is more abominable than the German; still, the German drunkard is unmistakably more stupid and ridiculous than the Russian. The Germans are pre-eminently a self-conceited people; they are proud of themselves. In a drunken German these fundamental national traits increase with the measure of beer consumed. He gets home drunk as a fiddler, and yet proud of himself. The Russian toper likes to drink from grief, and to weep. And even while he assumes bold airs, he does not triumph, but is merely turbulent. Invariably, he will recall some offense and will start reproaching the offender, whether or not he be present. Insolently, he will, perhaps, argue that he is something next to a general; he swears bitterly and, if people refuse to believe him, he will finally sound an alarm and cry out for help. Still, the reason why he is so ugly and why he cries out for help is that, in the innermost part of his tipsy soul, he is unquestionably convinced that he is no 'general' at all, but merely a nasty sot, and that he has become filthier than a beast."

"But I am a novelist, and it seems that one 'story' I did invent myself. Why did I say 'it seems,' since I know for certain that I did actually invent it; yet I keep fancying that this happened somewhere, once upon a time, precisely on Christmas Eve, in *some* huge city during a bitter frost."

"On Sundays, toward evening (on weekdays they are not seen at all) a great many of these absolutely sober people engaged all week in work, go out into the streets. Precisely, they come out for a walk. I have noticed that they never go on the Nevsky: mostly, they stroll near their homes, or they walk along 'leisurely,' returning with their families after visiting some people. (It seems there are also a great many married workers in Petersburg.) They walk along sedately and with awfully serious faces, as if it were not just a walk, conversing very little with each other, especially husbands with their wives— almost silently, but invariably in their holiday clothes.

"Their clothing is old and bad—on women, it is many-colored: but everything is cleaned and washed for the holiday, intentionally —perhaps, for this hour. . . .

"The most annoying part is that they really and seriously imagine, it seems, that by strolling in this manner they are providing themselves with genuine Sunday recreation."

From the Notebooks of F. Scott Fitzgerald:
"Then there's Emily. You know what happened to her; one night her husband came home and told her she was acting cold to him, but that he'd fix that up. So he built a bonfire under her bed, made up of shoes and things, and set fire to it. And if the leather hadn't smelled so terrible, she'd have been burned to death."

"We can't just let our worlds crash around us like a lot of dropped trays."

"In the deep locker-room of the earth."

"Days of this February were white and magical, the nights were starry and crystalline. The town lay under a cold glory."

"New York's flashing, dynamic good looks, its tall man's quick-step."

"All of a sudden the room struck like a clock."

"He passed an apartment house that jolted his memory. It was on the outskirts of town, a pink horror built to represent something, somewhere, so cheaply and sketchily that whatever it copied the architect must have long forgotten."

"The restaurant with a haunted corner."

Observations in this author's notebook after completing some short stories:

"One must have an *arresting first paragraph*. A fumbling, or too wordy first paragraph can tire the reader before he begins; worse still, he may miss some valuable information."

"Let your mind be *working on your title* as you go along."

"*Tell* yourself the story first, as far as you are able. But do not complete too thoroughly, for then you will have the feeling it has already been done."

"Try for *one powerful effect* throughout your short story. Jealousy: everything must either point to or away from that emotion, leading to action at the end. Irony: the inconsistencies—or unadmitted consistencies—of the human animal. An entire story could be built on this."

"Do not resist the suddenly *irrational* in a story: that's imagination at work."

"Find the *key emotion:* this may be all you need know to find your short story."

"Search for repetition of *words*. The mind has a curious obsession at times with single words."

"*Trust:* the *length* of a story follows naturally its development, if you relax. One need not be arbitrary about word length."

"*Pace.* Keep the pace, never let the attention wander. Like a public speaker, keep on talking even if you are not quite sure of what you are going to say. The subconscious helps. Anything is better than a sudden drop in temperature, a lack of sweat from start to finish, or at any point in between."

"*Tension:* must be held at all times in the short story."

"*Ending.* Know when you have reached the right moment to stop. Use instinct here; develop your sensitivity to the end of a thought, to the climax and its significance. This is no more than developing your wit. There are several lengths at which to snip off your narrative, but only one will fit *that* story."

*"Read back, read back, read back.* Go over work coldly, mercilessly for sentimentality, lush writing, grammatical errors, tedious dialogue, lack of wit, repetition, phrases and clauses out of place. . . . But also go over it emotionally, sensitively, *feelingly,* mindlessly, for that is how your reader will expect it to hold him."

*"Speak* your prose."

From students' notebooks, Sarah Lawrence College, 1961. Reprinted from *STORY:*

"When one is young and susceptible to poetic letters from delightfully neurotic young men, one must be careful to distinguish between those who write beautiful things and those who write things beautifully."

"Nothing is good in excess, including moderation."

"There is no greater fanatic than the man who stands solidly in the middle of the road."

"It's not that I don't like him; but when we're together, I'm bored with myself."

"Too many women I know are oval and round: I want to be a thousand corners, a geometric dream of squares and lines, corners never blunted, never sanded. I want to be a line that goes on and on and turns and moves to right and left and up and down and forward: knowing where I'm going, but sometimes going somewhere else, to some new corner, darker, greater, not a circle, softly twisting, mincing, this way, that, ending up just where it started."

Nancy Weber

"I am sitting in the room again, surrounded by things that have been in it my whole three years at school. There really is a large part of me here, although sometimes I have a hard time trying to find it. And then that wretched girl, who didn't understand, came in the other day, and said: 'Your room looks just the same way it did the first time I met you. Haven't you ever thought of changing it?' How could I tell her I hadn't found myself in it yet? I bet she hasn't found herself in her room; that must be why she changes it all the time."

"Change is excitement, be it for bad or good."

"Another long subway ride back to the middle of town. There was a woman sitting at the end of the car dressed from bottom to top in heavy black wool clothes. She could have been riding through Russia; especially with the babushka on her head, pulled almost over her eyes. The leatherlike texture of her face was everywhere covered with wrinkles and lines. She was so incongruous in that modern-day coach, beside the freshly painted teenagers, in their light cotton dresses, who stood at the other end snickering about a sign over their heads. . . ."

"We could *write* of that night, but it would never be the same as it is when we *think* about it."

Pamela Howard

"We marched into N.Y. all dressed alike—tights, black skirts, etc. . . . I don't know why we're here, although it is quite pleasant. It's raining outside. Dodo is wearing a wedding ring—I wonder why. We're all sitting here listening to 'The Man with the Golden Arm,' and reading love comics. . . ."

"She was so conscious of his physical handicap that she handicapped herself. . . ."

"The reason why it's nice to be an adult is that there aren't any more grown-ups around."

Sally Clay

"No desire is as pressing as the desire to desire."

"The plebe at West Point is like a gray rug with a black stripe: stepped on, crushed and dull."

Meredith Monk

# IV
## THE SHORT STORY

# 1
# SOME INTRODUCTORY MATERIAL

WHIT BURNETT once spoke to a class on writing: "I have no formula, no rule by which you can write a short story. Each short story makes its own rule, depending on the substance it has and the vitality; you communicate life to that substance and give form to it. All I can do is to hope that the few pearls I can scatter around will glisten here and there; or when you hand in something so bad that I can detect it, then we can analyze it to death. A good story is harder to analyze. It is a little miracle that comes into the world in your privacy, that you have written the best you know how."

Ring Lardner was once asked by a hopeful publisher to write a book entitled *How to Write a Short Story.* And finally he did. It was somewhat negative. Ring Lardner did not consider himself a teacher, but he did write short stories, and it is his stories people remember, not his advice that you should never write your stories on used paper, never write them on a postcard, and never send them to an editor by Morse code.

He concluded that the best guide on how to write short stories is to read those already published by any good author, and the best way to discover your own talent, if you have any, is not to talk about the stories you find swimming about in your head, but to write them down, and to keep on writing them. This is what it all amounts to in the end, anyway. And even though not everyone who has a typewriter can produce a publishable short story (having edited a magazine of short stories, off and on, for more than one generation, we have seen the results of such casual optimism), still the only way to find out if you are a writer or not is to write. For the written tale is not the same as the spoken tale, and the writer must, from the start, accept the limitations and fulfil the requirements of his particular medium.

Basically, it ought to be quite easy to write a good short story. The elements are so simple. Reduced to the minimum requirements, there are only three factors: the world, the author, and the end product of their interplay, the story. Between the world and the author exist attraction and repulsion, each acting on the other. As authors, we are always taking in impressions from our environment; we react at once to create the story, or we save experience up for later use, frequently swimming and twisting and even suffering in the process of acceptance or rejection. Either the world is too much with us, impinging on our precious personalities, or, from loneliness or anxiety, we rush out to catch it, fearing it will elude our fond embrace. We love it, hate it, fear it, select from its variety, and remake its image. And when we refashion, in writing, a kind of happening out of our experience, we may have, in the end, a story. No author has existed without a world around him, and no stories have been recorded, since the parables of Jesus, without the storyteller's gift. The bombardments of the world perhaps strike through the author more than through most people because of his receptivity.

"Oh, Lord," Katherine Mansfield wrote in a journal note a year before her death, "make me crystal clear for Thy light to shine through!"

With Katherine Mansfield and her Miss Brill, who sat in the park in Paris listening to the band—and that was *her* world—the circle of the world was not very big. With W. Somerset Maugham, a traveler as familiar with the South Seas or the Far East as with the capitals of Europe, the world was wider. Hemingway used an African world, a sporting world, a gangster world, a world dominated by wars; H. E. Bates, the English story writer, created a tiny world in a country pub where two old gaffers privately plan a fishing trip in a stream in which they will never fish.

Some stories, often the humorous ones, and those with overtones of philosophy, so revolve around the personality of the author that there is more the sense of a personalized middleman than of the world or of the "story." Most stories, like most eggs, are quickly laid, consumed, and forgotten; but there are those others that outlast the lives and even the names of their mortal authors. These are the ones Luigi Pirandello once called "the fertile eggs of literature," the ones with life in them which, when hatched, may go on and sire a line. Such were the stories by the Italian Boccaccio and the tales of

Chaucer, and the chronicles from which Shakespeare drew the plots for his genius. They are the stories that are so universal in their story essence that they can be told and retold. And some authors have had this force, fertilizing other writers to come.

But each author has his own world as his own possession to draw upon, with all its scenes and people in it. It is you who will decide, as far as you are able, on your particular potentialities, the things you want to say in your short stories. The task is merely to set the forces of your talent in operation, and to begin to write.

In "The Short Story from a Purely Personal View," I wrote for *Writer's Digest* magazine: The requirements of the short story, while substantially constant, change in manner and technique from season to season, and from generation to generation. Re-read stories appearing in most American magazines twenty to fifty years ago and see how they deal not only with different attitudes and situations, but are written in a style which now may seem florid, over-explicit, or, at best—as in the early and so-called 'typical' *New Yorker* stories—pedestrianly realistic. Go back another generation or two when a writer such as O. Henry wrote in a style which now one imitates at risk of appearing ridiculous; and before that, consider a literary masterpiece such as Leo Tolstoi's "The Death of Ivan Ilyich," which unhappily shows us more about how not to write the short story of today than how one should be written. Yet all these stories have that requirement set forth by Robert Gorham Davis in his *Ten Modern Masters,* the requirement that a story asks a question—"What is it like to be that kind of a person going through that kind of an experience?"—and then answers it.

How do you know you have a story to tell? Where do you settle your wandering and rather anxious imagination? How do you begin?

The prime test of whether you have a story or not is that you find in every contemplated story an *explosion*—muted perhaps, delayed sometimes, or completely shattering—but something which *explodes* and thus changes the status quo. Somewhere, either at the beginning, middle, or end, there is an explosion in which all parts of the whole are expelled from an existing pattern—the lives of the characters are jolted from their rhythm, and chaos is produced in their universe. Out of this upheaval, "that kind of person going through that kind of experience," the creative skill of the author must find or imply some sort of resolution: this is the true pattern of the short story. And the writer, before he begins to write, must anticipate and comprehend this explosion and then, without being guided by anything but his own inner logic, create—or suggest—new order from the old.

An explosion may be many things, it make use of any subject matter. The breakup of a marriage, the beginning of love, the death of an old man—each can create its own chaos, provide its own solution. The explosion may be used in three ways. One can commence with the explosion—in other words, the gun goes off at once, and the universe seems shattered at the point the story begins. It is then up to the author to reassemble the characters, lead to some final acceptance or solution in their lives, as in Mary McCarthy's "Cruel and Barbarous Treatment," where the marriage is shown breaking up and the story works out from there.

Or the story may begin with calm and existing order, proceeding with rising intensity to an explosion in the center, working back to a new order at the end—which, of course, is never quite the same as the old. "The Man," by Mel Dinelli (discussed in Part I), comes back to the same starting point, but the consciousness of the victim is not the same as it was.

Or one may withhold ammunition to the very end, as in Shirley Jackson's story "The Lottery," when the stoning begins and the full meaning of the preceding pages bursts upon the reader with horror, leaving him then to reassemble the parts for himself.

Any story, I think, will fall into one of these three patterns, and the author, by approaching the problem in his own mind before he starts to write, will know the moment in his tale when it is most effective to light the fuse, how far back to stand from the subject at the time of the explosion, and whether he is going to set it off at the beginning, the middle, or the end. An author can take his choice, and begin his story accordingly.

Once you start to write your story, the next important thing is to finish it. Writing is as simple, and as difficult, as that. An incomplete story is no story at all, while a piece of writing with all the faults of English grammar can be a story if brought to some related end. There is no substitute stage in your development as a writer for finishing what you have begun. I myself can clearly remember the day I became a writer: it was the day I stopped dreaming up ideas without developing them, and forced myself through to a definite ending. Even though that story was never published and has been lost long since, it was an important milestone in my writing. Then, for several months after that, I worked as fast as ideas came and, miraculously, the more I completed, the greater the profusion of stories I thought to tell.

Then came the next stage, when a feeling of uneasiness came over me as I went back and reread all I had written; and I saw these stories would have to be rewritten, and maybe even rewritten again. That was the third stage of my becoming a writer, and one that has never ended.

Below we discuss some of the principal types of story.

*Traditional story.* The short story, being short and easily under-taken like the narrative and lyric poem, is usually the first form of fiction which attracts the young when they begin to test their talents in writing. The first short stories of a beginning author (whether published then or later) are often written, as the first stories histori-cally and traditionally were written, out of a desire to tell a story—usually a simple, albeit absorbing one, its structure as uncomplicated as an incident or episode—a little moral tale, a parable, or an anec-dote. First short stories, which may be based on such unsophisticated origins, are often derivative of something the author has read or been told, whether he is conscious of this or not. He encounters something in his own background or picks up something he has heard, and because it strikes him as something fitting into story form, he decides to set it down.

*Subject story.* The next stage in the development of a short story writer is usually his discovery that he himself is a personality, perhaps even his own best character, that there are depths in himself he should reveal because he alone can best reveal them, and that he, in his own way, is as much entitled to be a protagonist as Marcel Proust or J. D. Salinger. While it is in this second developmental stage that many short story writers first find publication, this fact does not invalidate the theory that prior to this important subjective writing stage there were many stories (still perhaps in the author's trunk) which he wrote before he discovered his own particular soul. In this subjective stage of the short story, which reached a kind of peak with Sherwood Anderson in the early 1920s and is beautifully developed by Gladys Schmitt (and others), the author discovers that his own personality and participation can play a large part in a story and discovers his own stream of consciousness, in which, for a time, he simply must be the principal swimmer.

*Objective story.* The third stage may be that in which the author makes a conscious attempt to suppress his own feeling and view of things for the sake of a more objective presentation of his story and characters.

*Experimental and symbolic story.* The fourth stage is often the author's preoccupation with the story form itself. Here he begins to experiment with different approaches and treatments of his subject matter and his manner of presenting it and to search, perhaps, for less obvious, more symbolic, ways to evoke his meaning.

*Complex story.* By the fifth stage, the author has written many stories such as those he has read by others; he has searched his own soul for insights and drama and put his soul into the story so often that either he or his reader has grown a little tired of that aspect of his art; he has written straight "objective" stories about people just as he found them; he has tried experiments with Joycean, Lawrentian, Proustian, and Hemingwayesque styles and treatments; and now he finds himself writing on many levels to express the whole of his art and comprehension.

*Universal story.* From now on, if he has not wholly abandoned the art of the short story for the art of the novel, he looks around for stories which he hopes and believes will be so deeply felt and so widely applicable that he can achieve something of universality; he can even create, if he is lucky, a story or two that are nearly "great" —that, in short, have everything.

*Exceptions.* Some writers' careers are started by a wild cry in the wilderness, in all its piercing subjectivity; other writers are rarely or never subjective, approaching always with their eyes on the object; and others are simple tale-tellers, taking what they find and giving it back much as they first heard it. Still others aim at depth, complexity, symbolism, and universality from quite early in their writing careers. Thus while the editors believe that they have an interesting theory of the parallel growth of the short story and the short story writer, given the nature of the people with which it deals, the theory does not always work out perfectly in practice. But in general, short stories and their authors do seem to have come along in much the above order, together. Fortunately, the short story is such a fluid form that it can accommodate almost anything, providing that somehow the impression of completeness is achieved, that something of a singleness has been attained in all the multiple possibilities inherent in creation.

A simple tale with a classical treatment is "The Dream of Angelo Zara" by Guido D'Agostino, published in *STORY* in the later days of World War II.

It begins: "Unfortunately for Angelo Zara the dream happened on Saturday night, and on Sunday there was no work and nothing to do but talk about it. Unfortunately he had to tell it to Matteo (Big Mouth) Grossi who lived downstairs in the same building. But most unfortunate of all was the fact that he wasn't built for a dream of such terrific and far-reaching proportions.

"In the morning when Angelo Zara awoke in his furnished room on the top floor of the tenement building on Bleecker Street he was seized with a violent trembling sensation. He realized that he had actually been in the Villa Torlonia and what had happened had happened right before his very eyes and every word and gesture that had taken place was just as clear in his mind as the tips of his toes sticking out from under the bed sheet. He wanted to get up right away and rush downstairs to see his friend Matteo Grossi, the bricklayer; but then he remembered it was Sunday, and on Sunday Matteo had a passion for sleeping late. Once when Matteo's kid accidentally shot off his cap pistol before going to church, Matteo had leaped up out of the bed in a frenzy and held the child screaming out of the window. Angelo Zara did not approve of this kind of violence, but after all, a friend was a friend and who was the man without some failing in one way or another? Just the same he didn't rush downstairs. He sat in his little room under the tenement roof, dressing slowly and going over every angle of the miraculous dream. Now and then his fingers would pause on a button and his features would light with an ecstatic glow mingled with bewilderment. He couldn't believe that such a dream had actually happened to him."

Finally, at fifteen minutes after nine, in a clean shirt and wearing his good pants and his black Sunday shoes, he knocked on the door of Matteo Grossi's flat. Finding Matteo shaving, Angelo "blurted, 'Last night, Matteo! Mussolini! He die. In the Villa Torlonia he kick the bucket!' "

When Matteo understood this was only a dream, he wasn't interested. But Angelo insisted "such a dream like never before I have in my life. Ma, plain! Plain like Jesu Cristo, you face. Mussolini he there on the bed. He gonna die and I watch. On his face is a big soomprise. Like he never believe he gonna die like this. Great big Mussolini gonna die joost like anybody else. He no can understand—"

He finally convinces Matteo with the continuation of the dream, and the story goes on with Matteo at last taking it all seriously, especially when Angelo tells how Il Duce had offered him "three thousand lire for month" to stay there with him.

"For a few minutes Matteo Grossi was silent. Then his eyes spread like two peeled potatoes and he jumped up from the table. 'Is a dream for Ignazio Ferro. Come on, we see what Ignazio Ferro say.' "

Matteo Grossi becomes more and more enamored of the dream. " 'Where that salamangonia, Ignazio? Wait we tell that to him. He study dreams. I betch this mean something like never we can imagine—' "

When they spy Ignazio Ferro, his "squat round figure was propped against a lamp post and he was chewing a toothpick and twirling the ends of his huge iron-gray mustache. Angelo started to hurry toward him, but Matteo Grossi held him back. 'Wait, Angelo! Leave me talk. If you tell him you spoil everything. Is no dream for you this kind dream!'

" 'But it was my dream!' " And so the story goes. Matteo tells it all.

" 'Please, Matteo,' Angelo begged. 'Was you have this dream or was me?'

" 'Never mind,' Matteo Grossi said. 'Is a dream like this no belong one man. Is pooblic property. We in America here. Everything for everybody.' " And Matteo not only tells the dream but begins to improve on it. " 'Was a stink in the room like one million rotten sardines. And his face! Was no more the face of a man. Was the face of the devil who have lost his best wife.' "

They then decide to wake up Amalfio. " 'We get Alfredo and Beppo.' " They start off down the street, with Angelo Zara following behind. And they go into Amalfio Testoni's pizzeria, where they are joined by Alfredo, the butcher, who lives in the building next door. And they all have wine. By this time the others have taken over the dream and are all improving on it.

"Angelo Zara rose quietly from the table and moved to the door. Nobody paid any attention. As he slipped the bolt and went outside he could hear startled amazement and the two new voices echo in a breath, 'Where you hear this?' "

In the end he meets Flannegan the cop and tells him that Mussolini is dead.

" 'Ye've been dreaming,' Flannegan grinned.

" 'Me?' Angelo Zara said in astonishment. 'Is too big only for me. Was five other men have this dream too!' "

# 2
# FOCUSING THE FICTION MIND: DECISIONS BEFORE YOU BEGIN

ONCE YOU HAVE an idea of what your story is to be, compare it with other stories in your mind. If you haven't read any short stories in years, you'd better read some now, by writers you have loved in the past and writers of today. What have you to say that is comparable, better, or different? How are you going to say it? From what point of view? What mood do you hope to sustain, or evoke, what emotion does the subject arouse in you? As in "The Dream of Angelo Zara," is the story so vivid that anyone who reads your story can believe that it is true?

Is the subject one with which you are saturated, the background quite clear in your mind? To write a story one has first to "see" the story, to exert the imagination, then to objectify and separate the story from the rest of the life around it and from the author. To sustain the story's mood one must think the story, feel the story, and ultimately *be* the story. An author's characters must act through him as their interpreter, as little blocked by his research and indispositions and frailties as possible.

All art, writes Dorothy McCleary in her valuable little book *Creative Fiction Writing,* consists in separating one tiny unit from the rest of the universe and holding this unit up to the light in such a way that it will appear the most noteworthy thing to be seen at the moment. While the short story may be the "lesser unity," as Henry Seidel Canby called it, in contrast to the larger unity of the novel, still it takes a unit of time in the life of an individual and brings it into such focus as to represent some significant and truthful part of the whole. While the novel may embrace the entire life of a man or woman or child—or all of them together, being composed of many parts—in the end it may be the significant units we remember as against the final summation and larger view of the novel. The important thing will be to find your "unit" and to develop the skill of fitting it into the short story form.

If a short story is a separation of its particularity from the world around it, one of the earliest things a writer must learn is the separation of his thinking and his writing from the kind of thinking and writing he might be practicing if he were not setting out to write a short story. He must put himself in a fictional state of mind, examine moments of experience as usable material, characters as intimate relations of his own.

In a class of Whit Burnett's at Columbia University, from which emerged such different talents as the young Carson McCullers and Mary O'Hara (who began writing in the days of silent motion pictures and did not take up short stories and novels until she was exactly middle-aged), there was one dark-eyed, thoughtful young man who sat through one semester of a class in writing without taking notes, seemingly not listening, looking out the window. A week or so before the semester ended, he suddenly came to life. He began to write. Several stories seemed to come from his typewriter at once, and most of these were published. That young man was J. D. Salinger, apparently indulging in "purposeful reverie," that courting period of which Somerset Maugham wrote.

One cannot say how long this reverie of a writer may go on, but it is a necessary stage of development, particularly important in the beginning of a writer's career. Generally it is a subconscious process, in which the mind fastens on whatever is of interest, gathering other impulses around the original concept. When there has been a long enough time of mulling over, says Dorothy McCleary, you will know when the story is ready to be started: the opening sentence will write itself. And from there on, if the first sentence is what it should be, the imagination and the talent should take over.

So it is that one important requirement is that you think in terms of fiction, not journalism or propaganda or mere exposition; that the single, intense, and limited effect that is to be your story comes clearly into focus before you start to write. Relate this to the photographer whose eye has become so conditioned to the possibilities of his lens that all subject matter is framed in his mind even before he snaps the shutter. This is not to say that once the print is developed he may not find more in the finished product than he first imagined; so too, the story writer.

Each knows there are bounds beyond which he cannot go—a

limitation which does not apply to the novelist—and the best way to know this, apart from actually writing the story, is to become so challenged and excited by what can be accomplished within a limited scope that he does not think of the subject matter in any other context. A man who writes editorials every day becomes accustomed to thinking of life as one editorial; to the columnist life is a series of paragraphs. To you, as a short story writer, life should look like many possible short stories, and before long the impulse to give back what you've seen will be so strong you will find your fiction eye focused wherever the possibilities may be.

The professional writer will of course decide, before he starts to work, whether his material is best suited to a short story, whether it promises the scope and complexity of the novel, or whether it is potentially dramatic enough for a play. Norman Mailer said, in an eloquent letter to *The Saturday Review,* that time becomes so precious to the committed or professional writer that he dare not invest his energies in a project without knowing where it will all end.

The amateur, on the other hand, has this advantage: he can still take chances, risk starting in a certain direction, then change his mind and start over again in another. Even as he stands bewildered amid the chaos of life, with impressions, ideas, stories, and experiences all but submerging him, not yet having acquired the technical proficiency to recognize in his material its final form or the limitations of his subject matter, he may yet permit himself to make mistakes. Indeed, it is even desirable that the beginning writer not settle on the shape of things too soon, but use his talent as loosely as possible so as not to impede its flow. All he need be concerned about at this stage is the strength and validity of his vision and how it can best be expressed for some possible reader, how he himself will feel about rereading it perhaps some years from now.

But let us assume that the short story is the only means of saying what we want to say.

Edward J. O'Brien explained that at this stage, "all we require is that it [the concept] be solid and as completely realized as possible, that it shall be used selectively for a single effect, and that it shall not be too trivial to bear the weight of a story." And that it is, at this stage, far more important for the writer to discover how his own mind and imagination work, than how the story works. "Enlarge your sympathies," advised Joseph Conrad, "by patient and loving observation, while growing in mental power."

How then do we recognize a short story amid all the conflicting impressions in our mind? H. G. Wells dismissed the whole thing by stating that a short story is any piece of fiction that can be read in half an hour. Seán O'Faoláin asserts that it is "an emphatically personal exploration," and Chekhov said a story is a problem which a writer must solve for a reader—although many of today's story writers apparently feel it is not necessary to solve the problem at all, just as some psychoanalysts believe a statement of guilt is adequate release in itself for the troubled mind. None of this helps those of us about to write a story.

So let us instead consider the conventional elements of the short story, a form often triumphantly American, yet also happily English, French, Russian, German, Italian, and any other nationality one may think of. A short story must have:

A character or characters.
Action, a revelation of what happens.
Background, mood, and physical setting.
Focus; point of view.
An explosion, climax, or high point of happening.
A plot.
A point and a meaning.
A manner of writing: style.
The proper length: under nine thousand words.

These elements should cover every kind of story, even though in some the emphasis is more on one element than on another, and even though in some stories not all in fact are present. Yet in every story that is a story, something happens—sometimes no more than a revelation of an idea or a state of mind. It happens to someone or is caused to happen by someone; it happens in a particular time and spot; it happens in some sequence or order of telling; it derives from, or drives toward, some kind of explosion in its little world which gives meaning, cause, effect, and purpose to the story; and it is written in a style relevant to the best evocation of the effect the story strives for.

# 3

# THE BEGINNING

THE START OF ANYTHING, including a good story, is something of a paradox. And so is a high dive. So is love. To a reader, the writer must seem to have all the requisite knowledge of the experience, he must seem to be the master of the beginning; the end, with its sense of inevitability, should take care of itself. It is important that the writer from the first line be propelled forward by concentration on an outcome which has inevitability and logic. Your reader must be so held by what you are promising with your opening that he will follow the progress of your characters to the conclusion of your tale.

At this point an author might well ask himself—knowing that he wants to write, believing from what he has read and observed and thought and felt that he is ready to try, through character, event, and mood, to work out a story, relating it to some essential drama around him—"How then do I begin?"

Here, although sometimes difficult for any writer to achieve, confidence is everything. We must believe we can balance ourselves on that taut high wire of fiction, resisting pressure and distractions to create a gravity of our own; but this confidence may elude us.

Gertrude Stein knew the answer, at least one of the answers, which she impressed on a young American writer one day when he was asked to pour tea for her guests. In his timidity he nervously dribbled the tea more in the saucers than in the cups, and Gertrude Stein admonished him sternly. "When you pour, young man," she said, *"pour boldly!"*

Let it be observed then that if the beginning of a story has been poured as boldly as the reader will demand, the story should then go on naturally with the imagination, talent, and persistence of your demon easily directing it.

"After all," wrote Lord Dunsany in a preface to Mary Lavin's book of short stories, writing a story basically is "a matter of acquiring the reader's interest, holding it while you tell the story, and making him see what happened."

There should be the shortest possible distance between the mind of the author and the moment of putting the first words on paper. Instant contact must be established with the reader in mood, dialogue, arresting subject matter, or character. Some editors (and readers) consider the opening of any story of such vital importance that unless interest is aroused in the first paragraph, an author's chances may be lost forever. Editors, reading thousands of words each week, have no time for guessing games, or for simple kindness. You are the author in command, whether you like it or not, and it is up to you to take your reader in charge with your own promise of satisfaction and completion. If you could hold you breath from the first word to the last, you would have a story worth anybody's attention—whether or not it is finely written stylistically.

And remember, in any case, the writer has this undeniable advantage: he need show no one what he has written until he is ready, he can always work and rewrite later, and frequently his work is the better for it.

A youthful Truman Capote submitted a number of short stories to *STORY* before we bought one for our magazine—before we "discovered" him, as editors like to say. "My Side of the Matter" was written in the first person by George Sylvester, and the humor and style were apparent in the opening paragraphs:

"I know what is being said about me and you can take my side or theirs, that's your own business. It's my word against Eunice's and Olivia-Ann's and it should be plain enough to anyone with two good eyes which one of us has their wits about them. I just want the citizens of the U.S.A. to know the facts, that's all.

"The facts: On Sunday, August 12, this year of our Lord, Eunice tried to kill me with her papa's Civil War sword and Olivia-Ann cut up all over the place with a fourteen-inch hog knife. This is not even to mention lots of other things.

"It began six months ago when I married Marge. That was the first thing I did wrong. We were married in Mobile after an acquaintance of only four days. We were both sixteen and she was visiting my Cousin Georgia. . . ."

Obviously this tongue-in-cheek style was beguiling, and because the story maintained the same amusing point of view successfully, the three editors at *STORY*—Whit, Eleanor Gilchrist, and I—concurred in the decision to buy it.

To go on with the story, the narrator and his bride go back to Marge's home, where she has been raised by the two aunts, Eunice and Olivia-Ann. The narrator says:

"I swear, I wish you could get a look at these two. Honest, you'd die! Eunice is this big old fat thing with a behind that must weigh a tenth of a ton. She troops around the house, rain or shine, in this real old-fashioned nighty, calls it a kimono, but it isn't any thing in this world but a dirty flannel nighty."

"Mr." Sylvester is insulted, for his size, for his laziness, for his "manhood," and Marge is pitied and put in a bedroom alone while he (the narrator) is made to sleep in the parlor. The situation and the ending, in which the young husband finally defies them all by locking himself in the parlor with a box of Sweet Love candy he finds and refusing to come out after he has been accused, probably justly, of stealing a hundred dollars—all this carries out the original promise of the opening paragraphs with remarkable skill for the nineteen-year-old writer Truman was then.

Take "The Sunken Boat," by Robert Payne, a story whose beginning seems to have emerged out of the landscape, and yet gives us clearly the feeling of a mood surrounding the character of the girl.

"It was still early, and the mist was rising from the lake, and at the edge of the water where the moraine came down from the high mountains there were little creamy tongues of mist, but in the center the lake was pale blue, transparent, with pink mottled flashes floating near the surface. The sun was already shining on the white flanks of the Grossglockner, and as she rowed lazily over the lake, she knew it would be hot, so hot that she began to be afraid for her complexion.

"She did not know why she had left the hotel so early. She had not slept and she'd had no breakfast. But at the first coming of the white dawn, she had felt an irresistible desire to leave the hotel and swim in the lake."

Robert Payne has depended on his senses here to evoke the early morning atmosphere, to introduce his character, and to begin his story. By a sensual choice of words the background associated with the central figure dominates his canvas as though the colors were created for both the half-asleep mood of early morning and the vision of the lake. The "moraine came down from the high mountains . . . little creamy tongues of mist . . . white flanks of the Grossglockner. . . ." And the girl emerges from the misty surface of the lake, rowing lazily. Soon enough the reader will understand her desires, which become his own, to plunge into this pale blue lake. To plunge into love.

Consider the opening of "The Green Grave and the Black Grave," by Mary Lavin, and the first sentences establishing the mood:

"It was a body all right. It was hard to see in the dark and the scale-black sea was heaving up between them and the place where they saw the thing floating. But it was a body all right. The body of Eamon Og Murnan, a neighbor married only a year."

The fishermen talk of the "green grave," which is burial in the sea, and the "black grave," burial in the earth, and they know they must tell his young "inland" widow that at least his body has been recovered from the sea.

When the young wife does not answer the knock on her door, they bring the body of Eamon farther up on the shore and go to the neighbor's house, where they learn that the young wife, for the first time, had gone to sea with her husband. She was with him in his boat and has not been seen since.

The fishermen return to Eamon, but the dead body of the young husband is gone. But it is all right now, for "Eamon Og Murnan would be held fast in the white sea-arms of his one-year wife, who came from the inlands where women have no knowledge of the sea and have only a knowledge of love."

It is in the beginning of the story that we feel the concern and emotion of the two fishermen, which will later include their worry about the young wife. This mood, so well established, then carries them steadily to the ironic climax, the discovery that in reality it is the wife and not her husband whose body has been lost at sea. The first lines of the story have set a tone that is unchanging to the end. With an effective beginning, there is little that you can put in or leave out that does not contribute to the effect of a successful ending.

The incomparable Colette, who wrote without illusions about the nature of love and the relations between men and women, always plunged immediately into the heart of the story she had to tell. The long story "Belle Vista" has this opening paragraph:

"It is absurd to suppose that periods empty of love are blank pages in a woman's life. The truth is just the reverse. What remains to be said about a passionate love affair? It can be told in three lines. He loved me. I loved him. His presence obliterated all other presences. We were happy. Then he stopped loving me and I suffered."

The writer then proceeds to tell one of her most original stories, about the two proprietors of an inn in the south of France who seem to be lesbians. When a guest causes the death of their parakeets, there is a series of revelations, and the secret becomes known: one of the two women is actually a man. The couple is wanted for a crime some distance away. Nothing has been as it seemed.

In the beginning of Ludwig Bemelmans's career he preferred telling stories to Whit to writing them. After a time Whit persuaded him that this was a waste of talent, and so his first stories were written for and published in *STORY,* illustrated by his own amusing drawings. The first one, "Theodor and the Blue Danube," starts out simply: "Dinner was over, the room was filled with smoke and empty tables, the orchestra played 'The Blue Danube,' and a waiter cleared off the buffet."

There we have the beginning of the tragedy of Theodor, maître d'hôtel, who every year returns in glory to his native Vienna and pretends to be an important person. Unfortunately, an episode in his youth as a bus boy has marked him for life: when a rainstorm came down suddenly on the pastries, Theodor had been ordered to clear them from the buffet, which he had done, covering himself with cream in the process and being humiliated before a lady he had been trying to impress.

Now, back again in Vienna, older and masquerading as a Herr Direktor, he is treated respectfully—until one day there is a sudden squall and rain again falls on the pastries and the cream puffs, and Theodor, without thinking, runs for the buffet and tries to save them, losing his dignity once again.

Sidney Cox wrote that to begin a story we start with sights and sounds common to us all. "So that soon with no emotional language, you are summoning his [the reader's] feelings . . . lending out your eyes and insight . . . seeing how much you can make things that delight and hurt you come to life."

We must be aware of the emotional content of our words from the very first line of a short story, as though we were trying to enlist the sympathies of someone very important to us. A good speaker will frequently select one sympathetic face in an audience and address all he has to say to that listener, stranger though he or she may be.

There is the sense of an author making the listener understand in the story "The Warm River," by Erskine Caldwell, of which he wrote to Whit: "The writing of a short story can be a dangerous adventure. What makes it dangerous may be the misguided belief of a writer that he is obligated to tell a story. And, when this design is followed, the structure is sure to be a contrived plot garishly colored with the gaudy crayons of the topical and sensational.

"But the short story can be more than this. It can be the explicit expression of a casual feeling or a deep emotion when, in conflict or with sympathy, two or more persons act in response to the desires and motivations of the mind and heart. Although it is evasive and not always successfully attained, this is the essence of fiction that writers of durable reading seek to implant in their works." And he chose as his own favorite story "The Warm River."

It begins, "The driver stopped at the suspended footbridge and pointed out to me the house across the river. I paid him the quarter fare for the ride from the station two miles away and stepped from the car. After he had gone I was alone with the chill night and the star-pointed lights twinkling in the valley and the broad green river flowing warm below me. All around me the mountains rose like black clouds in the night, and only by looking straight heavenward could I see anything of the dim afterglow of sunset.

"The creaking footbridge swayed with the rhythm of my stride and the momentum of its swing soon overcame my pace. Only by walking faster and faster could I cling to the pendulum as it swung on its wide arc over the river."

From here on we have a love story, so sensitively told that one has the feeling of deep emotion. A man travels some distance to see a girl he is having an affair with back in the city. Her father is there; the mood is serene and warm. But when the girl comes to his room that night, he rejects her without quite knowing why.

It is not until the next morning that he understands it is because he has fallen in love with her, and wants more from their love than the sensation of this one night.

# 4
# THE SUBJECT OF YOUR STORY

YOU KNOW YOUR background. You know many curious individuals and the things they have done, you are aware of their little dramas, and you have seen them, or imagined them, in critical situations. And the simplest technique toward stimulating a short story is to take advantage of an exceptional interest in someone, to try to imagine what would happen to such a person in a different, more revealing setting. How would he face tragedy, disgrace, joy, or ridicule? Could some unforeseen circumstance destroy his equilibrium? Is he capable of intense love or intense hate? The subject of a short story may be as various and many-faceted in the hands of its practitioners as the personal essay story of William Saroyan's early writing or the fantasies of Donald Barthelme; the nostalgic tales of Isaac B. Singer or the psychologically perceptive stories of Bernard Malamud, Howard Nemerov, and John Updike. Indeed, as H. E. Bates has said, the short story can be anything from a prose poem without plot or character to an analysis of the most complex human emotions relating to any subject under the sun—from the death of a horse to a young girl's first love affair. "For the first time in English literature," Bates wrote some years ago, "the short story has become something more than a novel in miniature."

Somehow, somewhere, anything that one imagines has probably happened to somebody. And most of us write of the world around us, of what William James called the "back door" and the "front door" worlds of consciousness. There is only one limitation on subject matter: it cannot go too far afield. It must be concentrated in design and limited in effect. Elizabeth Bowen wrote that a short story, to be truly effective, must come from a direct and personal impression—a sort of psychological "flutter of the nerves." Yet that flutter must be limited to a single emotion in a short story, whatever may be its genesis.

An anecdote is not a short story, but it may be used as a springboard to a story. Some years ago we published a group of *Three Fables* in *STORY,* and the most amusing of these was "The Strange Notion," by Harold Helfer.

"It was on an October evening when I happened to go over to Jeff Stoneymaker's farm and first saw him lifting up the young heifer.

" 'What does she weigh?' I called out to him.

"He put the heifer down, took off his thick-lensed glasses and wiped them with a red kerchief and said, 'Oh, I'd calculate she's around forty-five, maybe fifty.'

" 'I know where you can pick up a scale real cheap,' I said. 'Used to belong to a veterinarian.'

" 'Oh, I wasn't trying to figure the heifer's weight,' Jeff said."

A week or so later the narrator again went to see Jeff, who excused himself and went out the back door.

"The heifer was there, near her mother. Jeff put his arm around the calf and lifted her up. Then he promptly put her down and started back toward the house.

"When he got into the house again, I said to him, 'Say, Jeff, why did you pick that heifer up?'

" 'I do it every evening,' he said. 'Exactly at five o'clock.' "

Jeff then goes on to explain that, since there is hardly any difference in an animal's size from day to day, "if I pick up the heifer at five today there's no reason why I shouldn't pick her up at five tomorrow." And that his hope is that if he picks her up every day without miss, then he ought to be able to pick her up when she's a full-grown cow.

The narrator drops in on Jeff every week, until the snow sets in and he misses five or six weeks. When he goes back it is five o'clock and Jeff suddenly gets up. Outside, the heifer, at least twice the size she had been, is grazing by a tree. Jeff still walks over and lifts her off the ground, even though now she "must weight at least one hundred pounds and probably nearer one hundred fifteen or one hundred twenty. And Jeff Stoneymaker didn't weigh much more himself."

Seems now Jeff never leaves the farm, for every day at five, rain or shine or snow, he goes out and lifts the heifer off her feet. And the heifer keeps getting heavier.

One day Jeff does leave to see a circus come to town. And when he sees a hippopotamus he gets a "dreamy, far off look in his eyes," and asks how much a hippopotamus would weigh. Later they go backstage and Jeff gives the trainer ten dollars to let him lift a baby hippopotamus, which weighs fifty-five pounds. The mother weighs seven thousand, seven hundred and fifty pounds.

Pretty soon Jeff runs away with the circus, writing back that he is an animal attendant. One card from Schenectady says, "I think I will be with the circus six years. That's how long it takes for a hippopotamus to get full-grown."

Three months later a letter comes from a sheriff written on circus stationery, saying Jeff has died. Seems he'd been practicing on the baby hippo when his glasses fell off, and he couldn't see without them. When he couldn't find them, he tried to pick up the mother hippo by mistake. "He died a few minutes later. They say he died of an overtaxed heart."

Before he died, though, they told him what he'd done, that he was trying to lift the grown mother hippo. He felt better then. "And he passed away with a smile on his face."

It is perhaps difficult to concede that a story might be written without any character at all, which is like presenting the philosophical problem of whether there is sound in a forest when no human listener is there to hear a tree fall. But take a charming story by Reardon O'Connor, "The Two Cranes," in which the author has written of two large birds, described and understood them, felt the perils of their existence, and related in story form what happens to them. The result is a story as interesting as any told about two humans, for in the final analysis it is not the subject matter that makes an effective story, but the control and talent of the author behind it.

H. E. Bates has written stories of great complexity, but he has also written tales so simple and lyrical they seem to have flown into existence like a quiet stream. "Fishing" is about two old men in an English country pub who, over the years, have talked of going fishing some morning early enough to catch the giant pike they know is hiding under the little stone bridge on the side where the rushes grow. One night, over a few pints, they swear to get up the next morning before dawn and do the job.

But the next morning—such is man's intent and his human failings —the dawn comes, and finally the sun too, and the little stream meanders quietly on under the bridge, flows on by the rushes, the pike, and the peace of the morning. And presumably the joints of old age, too, are left undisturbed.

Here is subject matter that might have come to anyone with an eye for character, an ear for misguided human endeavor, and the fictional wit to see the irony in the intention and the situation. Here is a situation that might have passed unnoticed by many writers and yet, now expressed, is a permanent part of the literature of the short story.

The short story thrives in certain periods of history, even though the same subject matter may be repeated and retold by many authors. At the beginning of a war much lyrical writing is done. The tragedies of separation; the quick developing into love of casual affairs; the feelings of a parent for the previously unacknowledged maturity of a son—these subjects require depth of conception and feelings, and poignancy of treatment. Sometimes an overall mood of doom prevails.

Later in a war, humor comes into human relationships and bounces up among strangers met along the way. Adventure begins to have a hold on the imagination, and a premium is put on daring. Love is a matter of quick sensations, romanticized attractions, of overnight affairs, and comradeship among men.

Toward the end of wars, there may again be the poignancy of partings, of love stories of men who had found a substitute for loneliness and now feel guilt at having left a girl behind; the soldier who has thought it would never end and now must make adjustments, uneasy about what may lie ahead. Sentimentality is too often the prevailing element in such stories.

We had them all at *STORY,* from Hollis Alpert's "The Lieutenants," a tender love story about three lieutenants who set out to have a good time by staying overnight in town, and end up going back to camp when they meet a pretty girl whose husband is going overseas, and has no place to stay with her—to Don Lawson's "The Channel Island Girl."

Mark, a young flyer in England, meets Gwen, whose husband is in the Air Force. They fall in love, but Gwen has resolved to go back to her husband, saying, "I am the same" as when he went away. Mark and Gwen remain just friends until their last night together, when they become lovers. After Mark is killed in a raid over Germany, Gwen remembers he said to her, "Don't you see, you can't ever go back to your husband and say, 'I am the same.' None of us can ever do that. It's not just a matter of our having each other. This has changed us already, all of us, this war, and our looking across a room and seeing each other for the first time. Or it would have been the same if we hadn't even seen each other. We can't go back, none of us. Nobody, not one soul in the world will ever be able to go back and say, 'I am the same.' "

Some years ago a party game was played by some of us which involved the question: "What do you consider the most important thing in life?"

The answers included many things: wife, children, lover, job, God. But there were unexpected answers, too.

A Marine on leave said, "The health of my rose bushes. I fed them some new fertilizer this week. I'm counting on being back to see them bloom this time next year."

A lonely secretary answered, "To be able to remember my dreams in the morning. I never do, and it worries me so, it sometimes keeps me from going to sleep."

The daughter of a congressman: "Never to have to wake up the morning after Daddy has lost an election!"

Let your writer's imagination place each of these individuals in a situation for a short story.

The irony of a Marine's caring most for his roses could be used in many ways. Suppose, after his participation in an armed attack on a village, he discovers that they have destroyed a rose garden similar to his own. Or a horror tale: he could come home from the war to find his roses blooming luxuriantly, but his pet dog dead from poisoning by the fertilizer. And anyone could imagine a love story with a Marine, his roses, and a girl.

The secretary could find the key to remembering her dreams; and the possibilities from there on are numerous. Are the dreams so pleasant that she thereafter spends all the time she can spare in sleep, finding her actual life uninteresting in contrast? Are they so monstrous, dreams in which she is pursued by wild animals, that she has trouble ever sleeping again, and what effect would this have on the poor girl's sanity?

And the congressman's daughter? Has all her life been a state of anxiety for her father's career; a career in which she and her mother are always expected to participate? To put on an act to buttress the father's image? Perhaps she has been frequently on the verge of moving away from home to live her own life on her own terms; but each time there has been an election to be got through first, and so she never leaves until—what then could cause the final explosion, decision, or action in this girl's life that she goes away, perhaps forever? Or stays, finding pride after all in having helped her father? Or kills her father because she could not escape?

The important thing is to let the story be told which comes to us with the greatest force. Once we find our clues for a story, after we decide on our characters or character to fit into its outline and their complex relations to each other, it cannot be said too often, we must plunge ahead and get this mood, this sudden crystallizing of our impulse, down on paper. If it takes confidence to begin a story, it is just as necessary to maintain confidence in its outcome.

For here other temptations may come in; the story may want to go another way, and, granting you have confidence in your concept and your capacity to realize it, there may still be a temptation to wander too far this way or that. So breathlessly—sometimes this sensation is a physical thing—slash through the distractions to that bright core of the story you know you have to tell. Follow where your instinct leads you and *get it down on paper.*

And if we are not entirely certain at this point what the ultimate result will be, or what the final meaning or significance, this may be all to the good. Ignore those writers and editors and agents who maintain that one must get it right the first time: second thoughts, ruminative thinking after writing a first draft, will nearly always improve our work done perhaps too quickly in the initial excitement of creativity. It was E. M. Forster who said that he knew his writing was going well when the characters themselves took matters in their own hands.

# 5
# POINT OF VIEW

FROM THE BEGINNING, of course, we know how important it is to settle on a point of view. Who tells the story? Through whose eyes does the reader follow the development and movements of the characters and the plot? Which point of view gives us most freedom, and which is most likely to add interest and meaning and sympathy to our story?

The apparent simplicity of telling a story as if the person in it were oneself makes the "I" narration seem most attractive to a beginning writer. And it is true: since the element of belief in the events we are imagining is first of all the most important obstacle between ourselves and our typewriters, it is easier to indulge in fantasy if we actually claim to be the chief actors in it.

In *The Stranger,* by Albert Camus, the author had to imagine how it would be to commit the useless murder of an Arab on a beach and be arrested, imprisoned, and sentenced. To be a certain kind of man, confused, as Camus obviously never was, and helpless, which Camus may very well have felt himself to be, writing during the days of the French Resistance.

The Arab was really the enemy of Raymond, the narrator's friend; but the narrator took his revolver away from Raymond in order to help him. Later, alone on the beach, again meeting the Arab:

"It struck me that all I had to do was to turn, walk away, and think no more about it. But the whole beach, pulsing with heat, was pressing on my back. I took some steps toward the stream. The Arab didn't move."

The Arab drew his knife.

"Then everything began to reel before my eyes, a fiery gust came from the sea, while the sky cracked in two, from end to end, and a great sheet of flame poured down through the rift. Every nerve in my body was a steel spring, and my grip closed on the revolver. The trigger gave, and the smooth underbelly of the butt jogged my palm. And so, with that crisp, whipcrack sound, it all began. I shook off my sweat and the clinging veil of light. I knew I'd shattered the balance of the day, the spacious calm of this beach on which I had been happy. But I fired four shots more into the inert body, on which they left no visible trace. And each successive shot was another loud, fateful rap on the door of my undoing."

It is unlikely *The Stranger* would have such power to involve us in the tragedy, or make us sense the heat of the day, the tensions between friends, lovers, and the Arabs met on the beach, if it had been told in the third person. But it can be done.

"A Painful Case," by James Joyce (from *The Dubliners*), is a Chekhovian story about a lonely man, Mr. James Duffy, and a lonely woman he meets "sitting beside two ladies in the Rotunda." In this tale told entirely from Duffy's point of view, we read how "Mr. Duffy abhorred anything which betokened physical or mental disorder." And how he "had neither companions nor friends, church nor creed."

Mrs. Sinico hasn't much either, but as their friendship grows, she invites him to her home and they spend long evenings together: "One night during which she had shown every sign of unusual excitement, Mrs. Sinico caught his hand passionately and pressed it to her cheek." As a result, because "love between man and man is impossible because there must not be sexual intercourse, and friendship between man and woman is impossible because there must be sexual intercourse," Mr. Duffy stops seeing her, avoiding all the places where she might be.

Four years later he reads that she has been killed in an accident, the account adding that her daughter said "of late her mother had been in the habit of going out at night to buy spirits." His first reaction is shock and distaste; but later, when he walks through the park, he thinks how lonely he is without her. "She seemed to be near him in the darkness. At moments he seemed to feel her voice touch his ear, her hand touch his. He stood still to listen. Why had he withheld life from her?" And he thinks that no one wants him now.

Two accounts of man's distress—and which is more effective? Perhaps this may be answered by the basic attitude of each man toward tragedy.

Camus's Stranger watches himself acting, standing outside himself as though he had no control over the forces which move him. Joyce's Dubliner scarcely observes himself at all and sees everything from within, looking out. One is in the power of compelling fate; the other creates his own destiny, which brings about the tragedy to another.

Both points of view are handled superbly, but since there is no self-pity in Camus's story, but an overpowering sense of guilt and error—and in Joyce's, no real introspection until the end, when Mr. Duffy suffers because he does finally understand his own loss—it is hard to imagine either being told any other way.

For the humorist who can relate the most outrageous things about himself, seeing himself not as others see him, but as both actor and recounter of his own deeds, the first person is an especially attractive point of view. Since the effect of laughter is what the humorist, from Mark Twain to Thurber to Perlman, is aiming for, the innocent, the guileless, and the bewildered character can be presented best in the first person. With humor as the ameliorative, the mixture is always acceptable. The victim of life's little ironies comes out of the reader's mind into all of us. His "I" transcends the self—his own self—and he is no longer the "I" of the story but the intimate, personal, and universal element in us all.

But however the author tells his story, he must never step out of character; he cannot withdraw from a role once he has adopted it. The reader expects to follow the guidance of the person who began telling the story, and he must not be deprived of his illusion that this then is how it all really happened. Whichever voice we choose, I or he or God Himself, we are committed to carry the story to its conclusion in the same person with which we began.

Textbooks on the short story speak of the omniscient point of view, as seeing all, peering into every mind, and judging every action. Even so, the narrator may not intrude himself in the action of his narrative; he cannot suddenly or ever become another character unless this is part of the plot.

Flaubert told Maupassant that "the writer in his work should be, like God in the universe, present everywhere and visible nowhere." Perhaps that defines for all time the "omniscient" author.

How do we settle on the point of view in a story or a novel? To go back to the beginning of this chapter: which point of view gives us more freedom and adds the greater interest to our story?

To take a story with several points of view which could not have been told any other way, we read "Horsie," by Dorothy Parker. Horsie is Miss Wilmarth, a trained nurse taking care of pretty Mrs. Cruger and her new baby. And here we have two points of view, which is what the story is all about: Miss Wilmarth's thoughts on the family, and Gerald Cruger's thoughts about Miss Wilmarth.

We see her horse face always smiling, being kind, romantic, and pathetically appreciative.

The young husband, Gerald Cruger, sees her as an interruption in his life. But he "had never thought of her having a mother. Then there must have been a father, too, some time. And Miss Wilmarth existed because two people once had loved and known. It was not a thought to dwell upon." So he thinks; thus his point of view.

Camilla Cruger is the center of their attention, and while we are told what she is like and her effect on others, we are not permitted to hear her thoughts. It is the contrapuntal action between Horsie and Gerald which continues to the end. He brings her gardenias.

"It was the last moment of her. He scarcely minded looking at the long face on the red, red neck."

To the end, Miss Wilmarth doesn't know what they think of her "as she looked at her flowers. They were her flowers. A man had given them to her. She had been given flowers. They might not fade maybe for days. And she could keep the box."

We may also use the narrator as observer and participant at the same time. Watson, in *Sherlock Holmes,* is an example frequently given to illustrate the advantages of a narrator always on the spot, but who does not himself call the shots.

There would be no record of Sherlock Holmes's triumphs without his paunchy assistant to praise and admire him, and to relate the circumstances into which they have been called. Thus we are taken into the confidences of Watson; we see a larger world than he would have created for himself if he had nothing to relate of Holmes's activities. And since not even Watson can see into the workings of Sherlock's mind, the suspense is at once his and our own.

The advantages of each form of telling a story are about equal. In a first-person narration, a character can reveal things about himself, his feelings and the workings of his mind, in a way a third person would find impossible to know, and which in the words of an omniscient narrator would sound less convincing. He can also carry us along as his emotions are increasingly aroused; and we might feel the growth of love with him, or sense, before he does, how he is affected by the heat, the death of his mother, the problems of his mistress, as in *The Stranger,* so that when the final act of murder is committed we are perhaps better prepared for it than the chief actor himself.

In third-person narration, we have a further choice: we may tell the story from the point of view of the main participant, a minor character, or several characters, as in "Horsie." We, as the author, can impose some of our opinions on any one of the characters—even invent one to express our thoughts—and have this one character see clearly the characters around him.

Finally, if we carry our point of view to the omniscient, we may know things, forecast drama (still generally a risky device), and perhaps focus on some point in the distance which will lift it all to heights above the story we have to tell.

# 6

# DEVELOPMENT

A STORY OUGHT to arrive as quickly as possible at a crucial situation, and then move forward from that point with increasing confidence. The author here builds up and dramatizes the working-out of his story line, tightening the threads and bearing in mind Edgar Allan Poe's warning that there should be no word written which will distract the writer from his established design.

If not in the first paragraph, then soon after, your story will have accomplished these things: identity of main character or characters; his (her) approximate age; his (her) relationship to the situation and to other characters and states of mind.

We will have suggested the immediate problem, foreshadowing the final movement, the crisis, the drama, the explosion. And we will have clearly evoked the mood of our story and the emotional and psychic atmosphere in which our main character functions. Now we must go farther, the actors must act, the place become alive to their presences. Something now happens, and we must move along.

"Stories are peculiar things," Seán O'Faoláin wrote. "Plot doesn't make a story. On the other hand, the absence of plot doesn't make a story either. In the really good ones, there is an inner plot. By this I don't mean the sort of thing—well, the grandma's will-is-in-the-birdcage-sort of thing—but a plot of character."

The story must unfold in the most selectively detailed way, relevant to how you mean to end it. You have not much time. The short story is short. But shortness, too, is relative. Once you know your own attention is keen, your attention high on what is developing, you may pour it out. Suspense in any story is what holds a reader. The old tale-tellers were first of all masters of the art and artifice of suspense.

Today the short story attempts greater subtleties and more candor. Yet suspense in one form or another is still essential, even if it is only a matter of how a girl will make up her mind, or a young man turn his back on his fears. It is still that half-revealed something which makes us ask for more.

If you look on stories as games of chess, you will see it is in the middle game, when the king is surrounded by his supporters and engaged with his enemies, that complications begin to multiply, and what develops here leads inevitably to his victory or defeat. Some stories, like "The Snows of Kilimanjaro," simply have the king beleaguered from the start, naked to his enemies, and the danger of his position is immediately apparent. He is checkmated when the gangrene sets in the leg, and the game is over. His queen has long since been taken, and all his pawns have fallen.

The really good story can never be played dishonestly, whether the subject is as innocuous as a little girl's birthday party or as troubled as the insanity of a lover. Nor can it be developed with anything but concern for logic, for a development growing naturally from the first premise of the story.

While you are writing, always keep one finger on the pulse of your story: this watchfulness is absolutely essential if you want to keep pace with the implications of your theme. Yet let the story sometimes surprise and even trouble you within the larger, surer framework of your tale. What if you did not intend to have this pretty woman turn out to be a bitter gossip underneath her smile? If that is the turn your story wants to take, find out what it means to your story, to the other characters, to your ending. Never follow a plan with such strict fidelity to an original view that nothing can happen as the story goes along. Writing short stories is not a daily exercise done with five fingers and a metronome. We follow a certain plan, but we must also, as H. E. Bates says, keep our imagination alive and in a "state of insistent and eternal fluidity."

Carl Gustav Jung wrote that art is a kind of innate drive that seizes a human being and makes him its instrument. "The artist is not a person endowed with free will who seeks his own ends, but one who allows art to realize its purpose through him."

Finally, before you reach the end of your story, pause: reflect; read over what has been written thus far. Pace a bit or take a walk on a country road. If there is rewriting to be done on the first part, do it now, before the last words have been written. But save the ending of your tale to finish in an hour or so, or the next day, since the story must now be clearly and irrevocably in your mind.

# 7
# THE ENDING

IN OUR ENDING, the key moment of our story, all the events and emotions and characters that have gone before will be seen to have had significance. Even if this is not recognized by the character experiencing the drama, we, as author, must now reveal what we have understood and known all along. That conflict in those series of encounters which created our suspense and seemed to lead in contradictory directions, perhaps confusing us and the reader even though we knew how it all must end, has now led to a satisfying conclusion.

But know when your story is done: use pure instinct here.

The ending must be visual, instantly comprehensible in the nature of the context of your story and, let us hope, provocative of further thought.

Elmer Rice was once quoted as saying one could reduce drama to its simplest form of development:

Act 1: Get man up tree.

Act 2: Throw stones at him.

Act 3: Get him down.

Now we must get our man down, even if by some difficult "dénouement of perception," as in Katherine Anne Porter's stories in *The Leaning Tower;* or by trick endings in the manner of O. Henry; or as Malamud ends his, in nearly all instances carrying the point of conclusion one step farther than his predecessors in the short story field have done.

As for the length of the story, if the concept has been right, that will take care of itself.

Finally, we will examine our story when it is done, for the balance of its parts, the consistency of its point of view; and we will hope to find that some basic truth, some supra-honesty and credibility, some fact of life otherwise obscure in daily living, will shine through at the end.

# 8
# SELF-CRITICISM

WHEN WE FINISH our story, or a few days or weeks later, we must stand far enough back from our work to feel ourselves no longer the author, but the reader and the critic; to work to some point of indifference where it will seem the story has been written by someone other than ourselves.

Here, unfortunately for the writer's personal contacts, begins the notoriously bad memory of a writer. At one point, consciously and deliberately, he learns forgetfulness—not memory—and even though he is in danger forever after of being late for dinner and dentist appointments, this brainwashing must take place in order to reach the next stage, that of self-criticism. For the words an author writes can form a groove in the mind which soon hardens and becomes unerasable. The trick here is to put the story away and practice intensive loss of memory. It will work, eventually; I found a few months ago that I could pick up my own first novel and read it with curiosity to see what actually happened in the end.

In this most critical stage of judging your own work, what errors do you look for? First, spots in which you have not succeeded in saying what you wanted to say, either because of writing too little, or writing too much. In other words, the balance of the story's parts is the first thing to worry about; and this, properly achieved, will often eliminate any possible moments of lagging, or letdown, in holding the reader's attention. Generally speaking, the beginning takes too long in the novice writer's work, and frequently the explosion, the big scene, is passed over too quickly.

Finally, we must find our title, which isn't easy, because here again there are no rules. J. D. Salinger started with the most obvious, and to our minds the most successful. Yet he wrote complaining that the *Saturday Evening Post* had changed some of his titles unforgivably; we had not. "The Long Debut of Lois Taggett" suggested just what the story was about, a type of college widow who never settled any place; and others we did not publish—"A Perfect Day for Bananafish" would interest anyone who prefers naturalness in a label. Hemingway's titles were good, and memorable. The titles that stay with us are not those taken from obscure references or lines from romantic poems. Here, as in all other phases of your writing, try above all else to strike that nerve of your deepest perceptions. Work on an association of ideas, and see if that isn't the only way you can come up with an acceptable title.

And the best thing, of course, is to have the title come with the story, without thought and without worry. This may be achieved sometimes by letting your mind work on the title from the beginning; subconsciously, one line from your story may stand out as exactly the title you want.

Finally, once you have found your title, for short story or novel, don't let an editor change it to something he himself has dreamed up. If you were satisfied with your own, you'll feel forever after that you sent your child to school in borrowed clothes.

# V
## THE NOVEL

# 1
## MATERIAL AND COMMITMENT

Yes, oh dear, yes—the novel tells a story.

—E. M. FORSTER

IN A SHORT STORY, success is measured by the author's ability to balance on a tightwire of total consistency, and on the tensile quality of that wire. In a novel, one's success is not so much measured by a flash show of control on a single wire as by one's ability to keep moving toward some ultimate goal in the distance on several wires, while juggling characters and plot and values at the same time, never losing sight of guidemarks or falling off. Yet in both short story and novel, every word and action must count in our overall plan.

For some novelists this sense of direction comes by instinct— talent, if you will. A necessary requirement of talent is also technique, gleaned from one's reading and a recognition of the elements of form and style—a process of absorption more often than of conscious thought. For many of us, successful work improvement may also come by trial and error, by which we develop a skill in self-criticism, and by which our fiction sense is further developed and explored. Above all, we must be able to tell a story in novel form.

How do we recognize a talent for novel-writing; what signs distinguish this skill from any other in the writing field? Not simply in the use of proper language, which is a requirement of all acceptable work, although the inclination to develop a thought to a larger conclusion, perhaps dwelling on the infinite variety of allusions to an idea, does indicate a capacity to take time to reach beyond the easily attainable, to travel that longer distance which is the novel.

Nor is it only in the ability of a writer to throw himself into his work and carry on without a break in transition; to develop from one possibly obscurely related point to another without losing the thread of his story, sustaining this the length of a novel. Nor is it that footlight sense which directs the inner mind outward toward all points of drama, highlighting patterns and images of results of human behavior in ordinary incident and event even while maintaining an overall unity.

All these things are important; but the novelist is recognizable, more than in anything else, in his awareness of space and time, in his sensitivity to the larger, more complex patterns of life, and in his consciousness of ever-widening circles extending to the limits of his imagination. When a novelist sees a character in action, it is not only in the context of a single illuminating moment, but in a series of complex revelations, and the paradoxes as well as the logic add up to an image at least as large as life.

At *STORY,* it was a challenge to recognize and encourage novelistic talent, sometimes after we had rejected a short story, when it was apparent the writer's talents could not be encompassed within that form and yet suggested something larger, something more than a small unit complete in itself. Other publishers wrote to our published short story writers, asking them for books; and sometimes, in the case of Gladys Schmitt and J. D. Salinger, among others, they had outstanding success.

But at *STORY,* Mary O'Hara, Turnley Walker, Francis Leary, Eric Knight, and many others either wrote novels without having succeeded first in the short story, or developed novels from the smaller form of the short story—a tradition as old as Christopher Isherwood's *Berlin Stories,* and as natural a way as any other.

# 2

## WHAT IS THE THEME?

WHAT IS OUR NOVEL to be about, and whom? If the novel has been suggested by facts or an actual situation in the first place, what other references and inferences will amplify our theme? If our novel is to go from *here* to *there* as a novel must, where is *here?* What steps must be taken to bring us to *there?*

Theme is a melody; the melody is our theme. It is that recurring insistence on the subject of our novel and the mood, with variations and elaborations made increasingly explicit by the actions of our characters and the plot from which these actions spring.

What obstacles, developments, surprises, dénouement, and explosions can deepen our interest in our theme and hold the reader's attention, and which must be avoided as carrying us too far afield? In the range and latitude of the novel, how can we be sure we won't go so far in our explorations that we find ourselves in danger of losing our way back to the mainstream of our theme?

What changes in the body of our story can we risk once we are under way, and which will further advance our tale and build to a final climax and effect? Do we find a theme first and then characters to fit our theme, or do the characters first choose us so that we work out plot and complications and suspense and theme from there?

These questions and others point to the necessity of learning, of teaching ourselves, of stealing from others, if need be, a technique. Somehow, before we start to write a novel, we must have absorbed all we will ever need to know about the shape, the balance of its parts, and what we want the final result to be.

*Technique* in the novel covers many things. It is, above all, that means of creating a conspiracy between the author and the reader with the skill of a Scheherazade, who was used as an example by E. M. Forster in *Aspects of the Novel*. The story, he said, was "the backbone, the tapeworm" of the novel on which all else depends; but this cannot be achieved without "suspense: the only literary tool that has any effect upon tyrants and savages." Scheherazade, he points out, managed to survive only because she kept the king, her captor and threatened executioner, wondering from dawn to dusk "what would happen next" in the stories she invented.

Commitment comes next in importance, and no novel will be successfully achieved without it. Commitment—which includes thought, cogitation, anticipation, and a sense of play. What is the spirit to get us through our novel, and will our belief and energy sustain us for the necessary length of days and hours? Are we excited by the prospect, increasingly absorbed in the subject matter and the story we have to tell?

The essential thing to remember is that embarking on a novel is not a trifling matter, even for an experienced author. If a poem is an arousal of the senses and a short story is a love affair, a novel is inevitably a commitment, and will take time out of our lives, our loves, and our energies. So unless you have the capacity to fall in love with the subject, with the novel itself, and with the process of writing it, give it up. A novel cannot be a careless thing and succeed in any way. The time and concentration, the quality of belief, all these and more perhaps we accept; but there are also lesser considerations in a commitment, such as revealing oneself to a hostile public or reviewers, or to one's family and friends, who may consider what we write an embarrassment and a betrayal. The price of honesty that we must pay is not small.

Finally, as in a serious love affair, we ourselves may find we are changed forever after, in some mysterious way, by the alchemy of character we have explored and come to know, by the experiences we have shared, the contradictions in ourselves we have discovered face to face, and the truths inherent in all revelations. We may be changed: we may hate it—or we may consider this too a bonus of the game.

For writing is a game, one of our own choosing, preferably played with skill and wit and intensity and the desire to win. Even though we may play with chessmen, by rules we will never be sure we know, and even though competition is keen—competition not with others but with ourselves, with our own natural gifts and indolences, our previous achievements or our failures, competition with the stuff of the novel itself, with the characters, and with a wayward imagination (even perhaps with a job which leaves us too little time and concentration for our novel)—still we intend to come out with a book in the end, and nothing else can matter.

So take time out for creation. Settle your affairs and take stock of your relationships with those around you. Arrange your finances and your sex life to eliminate anxiety and not to interfere with the functioning of your creative writing juices. Then sail into your novel without counting further cost, writing enough each day to feel a sense of accomplishment, of somehow getting to the end; dream the lives of your characters and doubt no more.

It is sometimes hard to imagine, at the beginning, that a novel *will* be done.

# 3

## *THE AMBASSADORS:*
## MORE BY HENRY JAMES

IT IS HELPFUL to recall when the impulse to write a particular novel first comes upon you. Here is where a notebook may be of value, of the kind kept by Henry James. He carefully recorded the genesis of his ideas and continued with a vivid expression of that further sense that a developing idea has on a restless imagination. And he carried the idea then from synopsis of a novel to the date of its publication.

He wrote: "Torquay, October 31st, 1895: I was struck last evening with something that Jonathan Sturges, who has been staying here ten days, mentioned to me: it was only ten words, but I seemed, as usual, to catch a glimpse of a *sujet de nouvelle* in it."

From this entry until his letter to his editor at Harper's in December 1913 and the subsequent serialization in the *North American Review,* he traces for us the development of his novel *The Ambassadors.*

The *sujet de nouvelle* becomes an American who is, he wrote, "virtually in the evening, as it were, of life." Which then gives James "the little idea of the figure of an elderly man who hasn't 'lived,' in the sense of sensations, passions, impulses, pleasures." But now he is in Paris, where "the old houses of the Faubourg St. Germain close around their gardens and shut them in, so that you don't have to see them from the street." James sees him as "this rather fatigued and alien compatriot, whose wholly, exclusively professional career has been a long, hard strain, and who could only be, given the place, people, tone, talk, circumstances—extremely 'out of it all,' has been heard to remark about what he has missed in life. 'Now I'm too old; I'm at any rate, too old for what I see.' "

So this, James comments, is the "essence and the tone" of the novel he will write. "They immediately put before me, with the communicative force, the real magic of the *right* things (those things the novelist worth his salt knows and responds to when he sees them), an interesting situation, a vivid and workable *theme.*"

This book will cover some six months or so in the history of the man no longer in the prime of life, and James gives him a name, Lambert Strether, and an age, fifty-five.

From here on James relates his plot in some detail, after deciding the American city Strether must come from. "An American city of the second order—not such a place either as large as New York, as Boston or as Chicago, but a New England important local center, like Providence, R.I., like Worcester, Mass., or like Hartford, Conn., an old and enlightened Eastern community, in short, which is yet not the seat of one of the bigger colleges."

Strether's purpose in coming to Paris is to take home a young American, Chad, to his mother who has been informed her son is involved with a Frenchwoman. It is to be Strether's duty to rescue him, since Strether is, for all practical purposes, also engaged to Chad's mother.

But when he meets Chad he sees "a good deal of rather fine and serious preparation for the event had been wasted." The young man is charming and easy to a degree, which in itself is a surprise. Strether is even more surprised when he meets the Frenchwoman, Mme. de Vionnet, and her daughter. However, it does not occur to him that the woman Chad loves is the mother and not the daughter. He writes this to Mrs. Newsome.

In the meantime "a lot of accumulated perception and emotion, seem to culminate for Strether." Mme. de Vionnet is charming, and he fully recognizes her as such. "She is young (that is, she is thirty-eight), bright, graceful, kind, sympathetic, interesting—and doesn't alarm him by being dazzlingly clever (which is the cleverest thing about her)."

And "there stirs in him a dumb passion of desire, of rebellion, of God knows what, in respect to his still snatching a little super-sensual hour, a kind of vicarious joy, in that freedom of another which has found himself, by an extraordinary turn of the wheel, committed to weigh in the balance."

There are further complications in the plot when Chad's sister arrives and gives Chad an ultimatum. If he does not return home within three days, he must give up his inheritance as his mother has threatened. In the meantime Strether has allied himself with Chad and promises to help him. Mrs. Pocock, the sister, and Chad then agree to let Strether decide.

"This is a summary sketch of what takes place," writes James. "But the thing none the less works out."

Strether takes a train to one of the suburbs of Paris "quite at random, scarce knowing, and not much caring, where he is. The effect of his complete decision is a queer sense of freedom and almost of amusement. It's a lovely day of early summer; the aspect of things is such as to charm and beguile him—the air full of pictures and felicities and hints for future memory."

But then he comes upon Mme. de Vionnet and Chad together "positively and indubitably intimate with the last intimacy; it is in a word, full, for Strether of informing and convincing things." So he knows at last it is the mother Chad loves, although certain events before have shown him it was not the daughter.

They return to Paris, separately, and Strether then receives a visit from Mme. de Vionnet which "gives her away to him—which is the last thing he had expected . . . the strange fact—of the passion of this accomplished woman of almost forty for their so imperfectly accomplished young friend of a dozen years less. Strether is in the presence of more things than he has yet had to count with, things by no means, doubtless, explicitly in his book; but—he sees and understands. . . ." Although he is not at all sure what he has supposed about Mme. de Vionnet "in his secret heart."

"Just a last sight of everything in her that he has found wonderful and abysmal, strange and charming, beautiful and rather dreadful, he thus finally adjusts and treats himself."

This "is really the climax—for all it can be made to give and to do, for the force with which it may illustrate and illuminate the subject—toward which the action marches straight from the first. So there it is."

Strether has sided with Chad; the Pococks return home; and Strether "measures himself exactly, the situation. He knows he won't make it all right. He knows he can't make it all right. He knows that, for Mrs. Newsome, it's all hideously wrong and must remain so," but now he feels that "his work is done, that his so strange, half-bitter, half-sweet experience is at an end, that what has happened, through him, has really happened for him, for his own spirit, for his queer sense of things, more than for anyone or anything else." He will now return home.

James concludes: "I should mention that I see the foregoing in a tolerable certitude of ten parts, each of 10,000 words, making thus a total of 100,000. But I should very much like my option of stretching to 120,000 if necessary—that is, adding an Eleventh and Twelfth Part. Each Part I rather definitely see in Two Chapters, and each very full, as it were, and charged—like a rounded medallion, in a series of a dozen, hung, with its effect of high relief, on a wall. Such are my general lines. Of course there's a lot to say about the matter that I haven't said. . . . The way is really, however, very straight . . . I need scarcely add, after this, that everything will in fact be in its place and of its kind."

# 4

# PLAN AND NOTEBOOK
# FOR THE NOVEL

WHEN THE NOVEL has been germinating in one's mind for a week, a month, or ten years, we come to the initial stages of putting something on paper. Many things on paper, perhaps, since we need to define our character or characters, to jot down bits of conversation and descriptions of faces, places, or possible scenes; even write philosophical thoughts in our best style without definite decision of where such thoughts should go. Sometimes, in gathering knowledge of a character, we *feel* the ideas he would have, cogitate with him in *his* mind over considerations which help us and the readers eventually to know him as he is. We authors grasp at any straw, pounce on random thoughts for further understanding which perhaps we did not even know we had. This is all part of the equipment and practices of a novelist, a sixth sense like a second breath which comes when we may think we have exhausted conscious thought and effort.

Obviously, the best way to begin a novel project is to have a paperbound notebook by our side and to put a working title on the first page. This, let us say, is—almost any title will do; a descriptive one is easier—a novel about a young student stranded in Paris. So much we have and little more at this stage, but we do want a title simply to give us that feeling (even though false) of at last being on our way. The title need not make sense, or be considered seriously in the end; it is likely it will not be heard of again. However, for this particular project, let us try: *Paris Interlude. Young Man in Paris. On Your Way, But Where, and Who Knows?*

After this we write our name: *Oskar Winterschmitt,* or whatever, but our own as the author, and *voilà!* we *are* on our way.

The next page, if we have thought our story through or have a firm or general idea of what it is to be about (and by this time we must), should be a brief synopsis of the plot. Since this will be torn out and replaced, perhaps many times, in the course of writing the novel, we leave several pages following on which to write subsequent synopses; but we start with *some*thing in order to further concentrate our thinking on a story now about to be formalized by the written words.

An example:

Young man goes to Paris instead of returning to college to graduate. He has read of Paris in the 1920s and imagines that somehow he will find it the same: a literary paradise. In spite of evidence to the contrary, he refuses to admit he's wrong, and every person he meets will somehow suggest to him a character from those wonderful years in his romantic mind. Even though reality does intrude, when he writes in his diary at night, or in letters home (not too many to be in the book; only a bare sampling), he will create a whole nostalgic world for himself. A nice American girl from Sarah Lawrence having her Junior Year in Paris, becomes Zelda stripped to splash in the fountain at the Tuileries according to his chronicles, after an evening he has actually spent with her at an American movie. French Vermouth becomes wormwood in absinthe; a hyped-up bum sounds like Verlaine. The novel to be about the young man's expectations, his experiences, and his gradual disillusionment, although the ending is not yet worked out.

This synopsis, it will be seen, takes less than a page. We leave it alone then, and go on to our characters.

Names come first, of course, and here we try to find names that *sound* right to our ears, names that *feel* right for the character, and that we *will not want to change* midstream. (This in itself can be a hazard; sometimes we change and forget to mark it on every page.) Henry James's *Notebooks* have pages devoted simply to names. From time to time he will seem to go on a name-writing jag: *"Names. Croucher—Smallpiece—Corner—Buttery—Birde—Cash—Medley (place, country-house)—Dredge—Warmington—Probert—Heming—"* and so on. Most of us simply dig around in our minds and hope to come up with one that has the right qualifications. Or look in telephone books. Or club lists.

The balance of a novel's parts must be considered very carefully at an early stage. Mark off the high points of your story and the approximate space allotted to them.

Ray B. West, in his excellent analysis of *Madame Bovary,* points out that this novel could be divided into the five acts of a play. "Madame Bovary is divided into five phases. The first phase presents the ill-fated alliance of the stupid Charles with the unbalanced Emma."

The second would no doubt be Emma's romantic attachment, which comes to nothing, with the lawyer's clerk, Léon. Léon, however, who considers Emma as a married woman to be inaccessible, goes away to Paris, leaving Emma, whose emotional nature has been aroused, once more bored with her husband, the doctor.

In the third act Emma, on the rebound, is seduced by Rodolphe; she and Rodolphe, a blatant and absurd champion of progress, persuade the clumsy Charles to operate on a club-footed boy, so that the boy loses his leg at the thigh; Emma goes heavily into debt for gifts she has bought for Rodolphe; and Rodolphe leaves her.

The fourth act would be when Léon returns, and a new love affair is under way.

The fifth is again her disillusionment, her turning to religion, and finally her death.

Henry James speaks of the novel's circularity, a description which applies not only to *Madame Bovary,* but also to his own works.

"Really, universally, relations stop nowhere, and the exquisite problem of the artist is eternally but to draw by a geometry of his own, the circle within which they shall happily appear to do so."

The last half of our notebook we will use for thoughts and notes at random. Bits of conversations that come to us in the night; dialogue overhead on a bus. Descriptions, again, of thoughts, of places. Intricate developments in relations which at the moment we may not find a place for in our design. Everything can be used in a novel, history, philosophy, nature, human frailties, natural coincidences, the absurd, the indecent, the outrageous, and the sick; any thought one has may be considered material if a proper place and time and hook in the novel are found for it. For the better novels, the great ones and even the good ones, are closest to life itself, and while the hand of the artist never quite lets go the strings—those strings tied firmly in our notebook of the novel—accidents fully realized and vividly or sensitively dramatized may give more meaning to the story we have to tell than the bare tapeworm of our plot.

# 5

# BEGINNING:
# WHAT FIRST CHAPTERS
# SHOULD ACCOMPLISH

MARY O'HARA once wrote to Whit: "Yesterday I could have said with certainty that I was writing a book—today, out walking, I said to myself that I really know too much to consider that what I am writing could ever turn into a book. I was surprised at myself. So there you have it.

"It might really turn into a book. Anyway, I seem to have got my teeth into it. It is more or less the same material I have been turning over in my mind for three years. I had planned that when I got over here to this little retreat in a country valley I would sit down and write it. . . . But as so often happens, when the whole set-up is ready, it bored me. Then one day, suddenly it sprang to life, the characters began to move. I was so excited I tried to write it all at once. (As a matter of fact, I have decided a book has to be written all at once, for how can you know what direction to take in the beginning unless you know where you are going? And how can you know where you will arrive until you see which way you are starting out?)

". . . Remember, at Columbia, I said 'write it in chunks'? I am working on the first chunk. Six or seven chapters. In the first chapter I have a grown-up young man hero. Then I got back to his childhood, and am enjoying it. . . ."

"Bring all your intelligence to bear on your beginning," said Elizabeth Bowen.

In our first chapter we should have place, character, time, and mood; this goes without saying. *Place* in the sense of establishing our milieu; a farm in Kansas, a hotel in New York, a colony on a Mediterranean shore. *Character,* as the protagonist or the victim, the thinker or the doer. *Time* is where we establish our beachhead, and our attacks range out from there. *Mood* may be the author's, or part of the characters or the times; it may change, be set up for contrast, be closely related to *time.*

In the first chapter of *Wonderland,* Joyce Carol Oates does all these things, establishing place and time as an element in the vulnerability and threat of tragedy in her main character, Jesse, a boy of fourteen. The boy lives in Yewville, and most of the town "is on either side of this street, Main Street—shoe stores, clothing stores, sporting goods stores, the bus station, the movie house, the post office in its fortress-like building, a few taverns, a gas station, a few restaurants."

The boy, nervous and apprehensive, grows more fearful when he sees his father go outside in the early morning in the snow, "his head slightly lowered, as if in a baffled blind rage, like a hunter."

Jesse goes to school anyway, the last day before Christmas vacation in December 1939. The author is very precise about this, because the season and its effect on mood and character and plot are important to the life about which she is writing. "There is a bouncy, hollow, drum-like urgency to the air. Jesse is going to remember this."

He is going to remember this because he is too anxious to remain for the festivities in the auditorium, and leaves for home to see if his father has returned. Home is seven miles away and he must walk, knowing there will not be time enough to return to school before he must report at his after-school job in a local store. "His heart pounds, seems to lunge in his chest. . . . He thinks of his mother: her light, red-blond hair, her eyes almond-shaped and clever and frank. He takes after her, people say, more than after his father. Sometimes Jesse and his two sisters are proud of her, when she is dressed up and pretty, sometimes they are ashamed of her when she talks too loudly." But now she is going to have another baby, which his father does not want. *His father does not want a baby.*

Jesse remembers a scene at breakfast that morning, when his mother's vulnerability was revealed to him. Earlier they had met in the toilet, both to vomit, she because of her pregnancy, Jesse because he is frightened. "Was his father hiding in the Brennan's woods? Sitting on a log smoking, tossing down the cigarette butts and grinding them out with his heel?"

The father is not at home, so Jesse returns to work. Suddenly there is his father standing in the door, angry and menacing, saying he has come to take him home, knowing this will cause Jesse to lose his job. And this is the end of the first chapter, establishing the character, the Greek quality of tragedy, and the beachhead of time.

In the second chapter, almost a continuation of the first—they could have been combined—the father takes Jesse home. Jesse goes on ahead, opens the door to a silent house, and "steps forward suddenly into the blood." His father has murdered the entire family, then kills himself, and only Jesse escapes.

From here on the novel is Jesse's, individuals who come into his life, developments and complications, until the theme and plot are relentlessly concluded.

Another novel will start differently, the theme less stridently presented. While one can no longer commence a novel with a long description of the moors, of wheatfields in which nothing moves, of the birth of an infant who will grow up as the book progresses, our interest and attention may be arrested by more subtle methods. Even so, no novel today can fail to present a promise of some kind or go long without providing the characters in whom we are to be concerned. Indeed, this is the means by which most modern authors court our interest and gain our attention.

Jean Rhys, in *Good Morning, Midnight,* begins: " 'Quite like old times,' the room says. 'Yes? No?'

"There are two beds, a big one for madame and a smaller one on the opposite side for monsieur. The washbasin is shut off by a curtain. It is a large room, the smell of cheap hotels faint, almost imperceptible. The street outside is narrow, cobble-stoned, going sharply uphill and ending in a flight of steps. What they call an impasse.

"I have been here five days. I have decided on a place to eat in at midday, a place to eat in at night, a place to have my drink in after dinner. I have arranged my little life."

The character is Sasha, clearly a woman who has returned to a place she has known. She is obviously trying somehow to rearrange her life.

She goes on to say, "I put the light on. The bottle of Evian on the bedtable, the tube of luminal, the two books, the clock ticking on the ledge, the red curtains. . . ." Later: "I take some more luminal, put the light out and sleep at once."

In the course of this opening chapter we learn (1) that our woman narrator lived in Paris once with a man she loved, (2) that he is no longer in her life, and (3) that she is sad.

She dreams of her father, a dream of guilt; then she wakes up. "I believe it's a fine day, but the light in this room is so bad you can't be sure. Outside on the landing you can't see at all unless the electric light is on."

It seems she has been very poor, and that she has money now. "Some money to spend and nothing to worry about."

But she does worry. "The thing is to have a programme, not to leave anything to chance—no gaps. No trailing around aimlessly with cheap gramophone records starting up in your head, no 'Here this happened, here that happened.' Above all, no crying in public, no crying at all if I can help it."

She goes to a café and observes another couple, and then she sits "alone in a large, clean empty room."

Finally, "a long walk back to the hotel. Bed. Luminal. Sleep. Just sleep. No dreams."

The end of the first chapter is a flashback of herself in Paris that other time. And in a few short pages we understand that the book is to be about a woman at the end of her rope, and that this is to be our concern. But since the book has been written in the first person, chances are she will be rescued, somehow, and that the conclusion of the novel will have moved us around the clock.

Forster reminds us that a novel relates life in time and life in value, but that there is always also a clock to be kept wound. We have set the opening at twelve noon, let us say, and proceed inexorably to the hour at which the novel ends.

# 6

## DEVELOPMENT AND HAZARDS. CLUES, LOGIC, RELATIONSHIPS

After having achieved our beginning, which presumably has been carefully planned ahead of time, we may relax somewhat. That is, we may adopt a mental state combined of listening to the story developing in our mind; of readiness to grasp the right words and impulses and directions when they come, without ever quite losing sight of our goal; and of cultivating concentration from the excitement generated by our awareness in the act of creation.

While we have a plan of prearranged activity, which we will never quite ignore, we will thus be free also to explore depths and meanings and relationships not quite anticipated in the planning stage.

Few novels are written in a strictly consecutive pattern, as we have seen by example in Jean Rhys's book. While her method of flashback is more subtle than most, in that she gives us the past as it occurs in a woman's thoughts generally without explanation, many novels make a sharp division between the present and the past. Erica Jong, in her very clever novel *Fear of Flying,* frankly goes back into the history of her past loves, past sexual experiences, and the couches of various psychoanalysts. However this is done, there must be an ease of transition and a logical development in plot, or consciousness in a character's mind, to justify the move.

It must also be remembered that a novel is not a series of short stories, that chapters are never completed in themselves. Rather, the technique here is *not* to conclude on a finishing note, but to suggest and promise that the answer lies ahead—in the next chapter, perhaps, although at the end of that chapter we are still pointing ahead to an even farther reach in our novel.

Some authors write the last chapters first, apparently as a target at which to throw their darts, being careful to miss each time but the last.

Anyway, in the development of a novel, it is necessary to fool oneself a bit, to pretend that I, the author, am as concerned as the reader about the outcome of my plot, and that we all have time to savor those intermediate scenes and problems as they arise. But it is only when I am sure that the full substance of a book is there, that I am completely in control—only then can I work this way and enjoy it. Then I can proceed with my characters as their behavior and as logic dictate, either putting them on, or getting them off, the hook.

Since the elements of plot must follow an uncompromising logic, so too must the development of our characters. In a novel, one may examine more than one side of a personality, and even explore contradictory actions. Yet there must be a consistency within the scope of the contradictions; fictional characters require the most careful and subtle handling. A loving woman, for example, does not turn from the caresses of her lover unless she is angry with him or tired of him, or has been injured by him; an alcoholic does not calmly turn down a drink if he is not trying to reform or trying to prove something to someone. A contented wife and mother does not become a vigilant feminist without some cataclysmic event or a long process of rebellion coming to a head. There can be many pitfalls in the long process of writing a novel, but the most important consideration must be to understand our characters in all their inconsistencies and paradoxes. Until we know how any character will act or react at any moment in his life, we will never be quite sure of the pattern or structure of our novel.

It is here we realize the importance of the point of view in telling the story of our book. D. H. Lawrence's *Lady Chatterly's Lover* would cast a different light entirely if it had been written from the point of view of the husband, whose thoughts are rarely considered in the development of the tale—or if we knew all that Mellors might be thinking.

An outsider used as an interested narrator may tell us something about each character and event, but while the omniscient point of view may give us more scope, particularly for a book of any length (in that the author himself may be there to observe, consider, judge, and present developments as the story moves him), these days it does not give us the latitude it once did. Philosophies and asides, as in the nineteenth-century novel, are no longer tolerated, and most books are told from the point of view of a single individual concerned in the novel.

Joseph Conrad's technique in *Heart of Darkness,* where a narrator tells a story in which he is not involved, is rare in the modern novel. We insist now on an immediacy of focus from the very start which must intensify as the story progresses. A novelist's chief concern must be on how to shorten the distance between narration and experiences on the printed page, to deepen the implication of the facts and faces behind the acts. And as always, of course, to get on with the plot.

Relationships between characters cannot be left to chance, or even to the simple demands of the plot. Yet the interplay between persons and their continuing or interrupted acts and wishes cannot be independent of all else; the actions of a character cannot take place in a vacuum. Some other character or characters must be shown reacting or responding to the major figure so that we see him in the round, and this is the responsibility of the author, who, by weighing his response on the side of the angels, will subtly direct our responses toward sympathy; or force us into condemnation by the control he has over his material.

Anna Karenina affected the lives of many persons, but in the end it was she who was judged and who finally must judge and punish herself. Tolstoi did not present the woman on a pedestal, standing alone, but involved with others, particularly her lover.

# 7

## CRISIS AND CRISES:
## THE USE OF SUSPENSE
## AND EMOTIONAL COLOR

IN THE JEAN RHYS NOVEL there are two love affairs, one in the past and one presently developing. One crisis is superimposed on the other; when Sasha is attracted to the second man, thoughts of the first enter in, and depressions and suspicions relevant to the past create shadows in the present. A crisis *enacted in her memory* corresponds to the pending crisis in her new relationship, and this continues to the end of the novel, a contest which creates crises, suggests ambiguities and contradictions that provide a basically simple love story with inescapable drama.

Sasha has sent her would-be lover away, angry, but then she thinks, "Come back, come back, come back!"—knowing he will not, that she has insulted him, and that she will now forever be left alone. Still, she imagines his returning, sees him out on the streets of Paris, coming into the hotel, up the stairs, until:

"He comes in. He shuts the door after him.

"I lie very still, with my arm over my eyes. As still as if I were dead."

But has the lover actually come back, or is this again a trick of memory relating to the lover she'd known before?

"The historian records," says Forster, "but the novelist must create."

The novelist must create suspense in the form of crises, having the power to mystify us as he chooses, but never can he forget to keep the reader questioning; always the author must be one step ahead of the reader and know answers which the reader may only guess.

Yet while a writer need not in the end tell all he knows about his characters, he must somehow convince the reader that he could if he would. He must give hints continually in his work by means of the colors of his talent.

Actual colors are helpful in expressing emotions, placing emphasis where human behavior becomes exceptional. The use of red—red face, fire in the eyes, and the like—will express anger, or possibly embarrassment. Green is a color which tranquilizes on a summer day; and the late Louis Bromfield, in a long-ago novel, spoke of an aura of color around the heads of his characters, which somehow added to their individualization and gave clues to their behavior. Research has been done by experts to determine moods expressed in colors, the various results being used in advertising to attract the eye of a buyer. So the novelist may add depth and convey meaning if he himself sees a scene as natural as the life before him, contrasted in tone and shade and values of the color spectrum.

Suspense may come in shades of gray, or it may appear as a contradictory flame against a blackening sky. But suspense is of course compounded of other senses than sight. Suspense is also sound.

In a wooded area we hear a hissing and our senses are alerted. A rattlesnake would make that noise, so we tread more carefully, looking, listening, even smelling (it's the copperhead that smells of cucumbers). We feel the earth harden under our feet and know we are approaching rocky ground; we recall that the breeding preference of rattlesnakes is under piles of rocks. We see movement beneath a boulder and then a poisonous tongue slashing out from a wedge-shaped head, a flash of stripes on a long snake's body. We feel fear and are aware of the color all around: the color of the snake, the gray of the boulder, the brown of the dead leaves on the path, the blue sky and white clouds beyond.

In our fiction we might stop here for a bit. The lady or the tiger? Do we try to kill the snake or do we turn and flee, hoping no partner to that snake will be coiled on the path we'll follow home? Maybe a tree has fallen on the path the instant before and we must go back around those snake rocks?

And so we also have suspense, which the writer will feel as he creates, and which he hopes the reader will be affected by as he reads. Suspense which keeps us asking, What comes next, and when?

In the novel, suspense created by ourselves must be a recurring thing, because our way goes past many boulders, retreats down many paths. Man may be escaping along the shore of a wilderness river, as in James Dickey's *Deliverance,* finding that once one obstacle is passed, another lies just ahead. Danger threatens in the guise of an animal, a torrent, another human being. Suspense may be overt as in *Deliverance,* or subdued, subtle, covert as in *Good Morning, Midnight,* or Tennessee Williams's *The Roman Spring of Mrs. Stone.* For Tennessee, each word is beautifully weighted with the possibility of contradiction, of disaster, of dissolution. In the hands of a trained dramatist or a skilled novelist we are kept hoping, or fearing, or plotting. We are kept in a state of suspense.

# 8

# INTERRUPTIONS:
# BLOCKS, DRIVE

THE NOVELIST with the capacity to see clearly from beginning to end before he starts to write, no doubt has the easier job. It is possible he does not have the most fun, however, and it is also possible that he allows himself to be so satisfied with his foolproof plan and outline that some spontaneity, and that element of surprise which can refresh author and reader alike, may be absent.

Sometimes the bare bones of an outline beg to be fleshed out, and it is a simple matter and pleasant indeed to sit down to a subject noted only by the words, say, "Party at the professor's house." And then write fully, with the dialogue, the characters, the food, the drinks, the conflicts we have intended in our outline, all responding to the more leisurely pace we can afford at this stage of our creating.

Then sometimes we put down bare facts, but find we've lost the drive and the fresh impressions of the original note. This can happen in the middle of a work, and it can unhappily result in the phrase "writer's block."

The writer knows where he is, where he has been, and where he hopes to be going; but beyond the bare facts used to tell it all, his writing juices seem to have run dry. There are some authors who reach this stage and never go beyond it.

When this happens, put the work aside, dream about it, think about it, but seldom talk about it unless you have someone so sympathetic and understanding his thoughts will work as hard at the problem as your own. But if you do not talk about it, sometimes, like the mathematician's answer to his equation, it may come right in the night and set you off again; or it may not.

A block may come at times to any of us, for more reasons than can be counted here, reasons that are not always as complex as they seem. Boredom: sometimes we find we no longer care enough about a scene or a character we'd earlier planned to write about, that we simply cannot put our mind on it with any intensity. Or perhaps deep down we know this scene is not really necessary, that we have already said enough on that particular subject without going into it again. Or a scene may be approached from another angle, told about by another person, than the one we'd planned earlier.

Perhaps we have been forcing ourselves beyond the point our muscles can take it; as with an athlete who goes off his game, a period of rest may actually be essential until the muscles have caught up with our intentions. So what do we do then?

The best solution is to skip on in your novel to another point in the distance. *Somewhere*, with a break in your mind's continuity. Think over the area you mean to cover, the scenes up front you know you are going to write eventually, and select the one that excites you most, that comes most fully and vividly to mind without your half-trying, and write that one, pushing all else from your mind.

For me, the most effective cure is simply to skip, to leave large white spaces, even pages, and go on beyond the point of interruption. Sometimes far beyond, to another setting, another mood, another point in the plot. We can always come back where we left off, but oddly enough, frequently we find that no more than a line of transition is needed where we'd thought many paragraphs would be required.

Finally, you may be censoring yourself; perhaps you would prefer writing more revealingly than your natural reticence will allow. There's no real cure for this, for your own nature does hold the limit of your work in the end.

Mark Twain, whose personal tragedies for a long period prevented the free flow of his talent, wrote: "As long as a book would write itself, I was a faithful and interested amanuensis and my industry did not flag; but the minute the book tried to shift to my head the labor of contriving its situations, inventing its adventures, and conducting its conversations I put it away and dropped it out of my mind. . . . The reason was very simple . . . my tank had run dry; the story . . . could not be wrought out of nothing." But six years after writing this he produced *The Adventures of Huckleberry Finn*.

Certain kinds of reading may stimulate our own urge to write, unlock the door that keeps us from our muse. Over the years a writer should have found his source of stimulation in certain writers if not in others. The early, lighter Aldous Huxley was for me a fertilizing force, as was D. H. Lawrence, particularly in his novels. For Whit, imagination could always be rekindled by rereading *Don Quixote,* although he complained the temptation then was to keep on reading, to not bother to write anymore.

A foreign language may help limber up the creative energies; or it may be a hindrance. If your attention has a tendency to wander, the act of language concentration may sharpen your wits, suggest new ways of seeing things. On the other hand, the study may become so pleasant in itself, you are distracted again from the writing to be done.

The most familiar trick for ensuring a continuing hold on your material is to end work each day just short of what is in your mind to write, to leave for the next day a significant development, a scene you have quite clearly in mind. Many writers do this, so that they are eager to get started on the next stint, without the anxiety that may come if they are not sure of their direction or wonder which step to take first. Also, in this way the drive has not been allowed to slacken, because there is a promise of writing pleasure that lies ahead.

# 9

# ENDING

"A NOVEL must give a sense of permanence as well as a sense of life," says E. M. Forster. And the length of the novel may depend on the time it takes to achieve these requirements.

We may have the exact point of leaving off, knowing where we mean to take our story before we begin. We may even stick to this, and again we may find that the point is inconclusive and that the story as now written demands we go one step beyond. Or two steps. Or maybe we need not go as far; perhaps we can end the book more gracefully by leaving out the explicitness of our original scheme.

Chances are we know generally where we want to go, and that this is approximately where we will stop. A story rounds out at a certain point; then again, an added touch of irony, or information, or projection in the future may be needed to complete our larger conception of the theme, or to decide the fate of our characters.

In Sinclair Lewis's *Elmer Gantry,* it would be interesting to know if the author intended the final ironic paragraph when he had his first concept of the novel. The book, remember, is about an ambitious small-city preacher, flawed by vanity and dishonesty, and the course of his career through temptations he does not resist. In the end, he has been chastened, perhaps reformed—but then he sees a new and pretty face in his new congregation, and one knows the temptation will not be resisted in spite of the lessons he is supposed to have learned.

But the novel is complete without this final irony; it is only an added bit of invention which does no harm and completes the picture of a character as Lewis wanted us to know him.

In my novel *This Heart, This Hunter,* the ending was planned for much earlier in the novel. In this story of a marriage, the young wife had forgiven her husband much, had stood up for him against antagonisms and condemnations from others, and in the end after she has left him and taken him back, there is a final scene. The marriage would go on, but—

Victor, the husband, sees her in her mother's home and wants to stay with her. But the young wife says no, she wants to be alone.

"Now even her mother looked startled. But after a pause she said, 'Then you shall, darling. Victor will understand.'

"A depression fell upon Victor greater than he had known in a long time. What could he do? His hands were tied. He did not know how to take a stand against these two women, and one was his wife, carrying his child. He had his rights, but how could he enforce them? 'I thought you might like to have me, Felix,' he said, trying once more, but not very confidently. 'You could go on to bed, and I could come up later. We could take a nice drive tomorrow.'

" 'No,' said the girl. 'Goodnight, Vic. . . . I'll try to come back in time for the Senator's weekend. I promise.' Dutifully then, like a child, she came over and offered her cheek to each of them for kisses.

"Her mother did not interfere but remained watchful, waiting for what either might do or say. He had to take it. But if Felicia did not come back in time, then the Senator would want to know why, and his whole future, the months of work he'd put in, the adjustments he'd had to make to accept their kind of life—everything would be wasted. Just when things looked like they might be good and stay that way he'd have to start over again, in some other place. Unknown.

"It was up to Felicia. Good God, and he was the one never going to let a woman tell him what to do. Now she, with her pretty ways and her nice manners, could wreck everything. Still, if she did come back, he knew what he wanted now, what he wanted to do. He wanted power and money, and he would have it, if things worked out at all.

"If Felicia came back. . . ."

Several critics spoke well of that ending.

# 10
## REWRITING AND HIGHLIGHTING

EACH BOOK SHOULD be rewritten at least once by the author's hand, and typed by him as well in its entirety. Highly professional writers claim they can give over a manuscript to a typist and worry no more about it. They are the fortunate ones, and sometimes they are mistaken. There is no substitute for reexamining your work in the same privacy as in the writing of it, rewriting some parts again and again. Novelist Frank Yerby says that "it is my contention that a really great novel is made with a knife and not a pen. A novelist must have the intestinal fortitude to cut out even the most brilliant passage so long as it doesn't advance the story."

In the writing of a novel, it is not likely that our interest and inspiration will be unfailingly consistent; sometimes we see deeper into a character and his actions than at other times. Sometimes we write from fatigue, and do not hold our strings as taut—a fault we may discover in a second stage. And unless the strings which make our puppets dance remain unslackened, the figures may collapse and illusion will be lost. The author can never forego his role as manipulator, whether he writes as one knowing all or as a participant; but when he does fail to create the complete illusion, he had better find it out for himself before a critic comes at his work with a fresh mind and perhaps an unfriendly eye.

Sometimes the trouble is not that we have gone slack at any point, but rather that the sequences are out of order. The story and material are there in the proper proportions, but we have put the cart before the horse, perhaps by introducing a character before there is a role for him, or by describing a place in someone's mind when it would be better left to the moment of actually coming upon it. Blessedly the writer has this advantage: no one may be permitted to judge his work until he is ready to expose it.

Our final and most sensitive check will be to read the whole of our work, sitting back and letting the complete thing come before us. After this we think it all over, and perhaps see other changes needed. We may need to rewrite large chunks, rearranging those episodes that seem out of place, using our knife to amputate in places, always being careful that the amputation does not show. In this context it is generally not enough simply to rewrite a line or a paragraph here or there; nearly always we must start *before* the rupture or the correction and carry *beyond.* There is a kind of heartbeat in any successful work, and unless this rhythm is carried through the amputation, rough moments of transition may also show.

But at some time your book must be done, and given to a reader.

Perhaps it is at this stage that we should quote the English critic Sydney Smith: "The main question as to a novel is—did it amuse? were you surprised at dinner coming so soon? did you mistake eleven for ten? and twelve for eleven? were you too late to dress? and did you sit up beyond the usual hour? If a novel produces these effects, it is good; if it does not—story, language, love, scandal itself cannot save it. It is only meant to please; and it must do that or it does nothing."

# 11
## THE SCIENCE FICTION NOVEL

SINCE THE COMMITMENT, length, and rules—loose as these may be —for all novel writing fall essentially within the same boundaries, we have not undertaken to categorize types of novels in this chapter. To an editor, if not to a writer, there is little difference in the requirements of a longer work of fiction; material, theme, plot, beginning, development, crises (one definitive), and the ending, mark them all.

Briefly, there are Gothic, mystery, adventure, crime, romance, historical, and Western novels, and "literary events," each having an important place in the tastes of the reading public. And there is the science fiction novel, which has been developed so brilliantly since the days of H. G. Wells and Jules Verne. Fictional prophecy has become a commonplace and accepted thing in the hands of Clarke, Asimov, Brunner, and many other imaginative writers. But it is something only an expert—in this case, two experts—can write intelligently about. I am therefore much indebted to Jack Dann and Gardner R. Dozois, well known sf writers, for the following helpful contribution to this book:

Science fiction is a shotgun marriage of the fantastic with the realistic. It is concerned with exploring man and his environment, as is any literature; but it is also concerned with how man will affect, and be affected by, his technology, new concepts and ideas, and other sentient beings, either man-made or alien. Using the perspective of distant time and space to mirror the present, the science fiction writer extrapolates possible futures, then turns them into imaginative experience. He makes of them detailed "thought-models" which reveal the soul of man through his reactions to old and new stimuli and which express his ideas, hopes, and *possibilities* in terms of dramatic process. And through this process he creates new mythologies. All human experience, science, history, and philosophy is used to create new histories.

But the fantastic and extrapolative elements of science fiction cannot be cobbled out of undirected imagination. "Anything goes" will not wash as science fiction, for after the initial creative burst—that intuition that a story is "out-there"—it must be fleshed out and made real. The writer must then work out his plans as if he were an architect: How far in the future does the story take place? If it is a different world from Earth, what are its flora and fauna? What of its history and culture and people? Before he can even get to his story, to the interactions of character, he must invent a world of detail, a world that is consistent in itself and does not contradict what is presently known—unless the writer explains why. One of the basic differences between science fiction and mainstream fiction is that the writer begins with a blank slate: he must make up his story environment out of whole cloth, imagine a consistent world of logical details which will make his story live, and then create characters consistent with that background who will interact with and in the world he has created.

However, it would be misleading to imply that the writer must be a scientist or have a degree in physics in order to write science fiction. It would be a help, of course, but what really counts is the writer's knowledge of people and of the craft of fiction writing, as in any other genre, *plus* the ability clearly to perceive the world around him and to extrapolate from what he sees. He must be able to perceive the hidden relationships that most would *not* see, to pinpoint the trends just emerging in the present which might become prominent in the future. It is important that the writer be able to grasp what technology does to us now, and how it does it, in order to come up with a progress report about the future of human condition. Remember that science fiction not only depicts new technologies and their effects but how people react differently *to each other* because of technology.

Most importantly, before the writer tries to write science fiction, he must read it; he must get an idea of the state of the art. The problem is that most writers who first attempt to write science fiction waste much time and effort unknowingly covering old ground, rehashing old ideas and material in wearily familiar ways. Science fiction has gradually established a language of commonly accepted ideas, concepts, and terminology, and the only way for the writer to become conversant with that language is to examine what other writers have done with it. Otherwise he may waste much time trying to explain the concept of time travel to an audience already familiar with the idea and waiting for him to do something new with it. In this respect, it also helps to be able to research (in order to lend authenticity to the writer's own theories, and to provide him with new ideas) books on science, history, anthropology, biology, and mythology. Any learning is grist for the mill. It may also help to subscribe to some of the less technical scientific digests, like *Science News,* in order to keep up with new advances.

Science fiction is an open-ended genre, a forward-looking literature that must be constantly fueled by new inputs of knowledge and experience. Once you have acquired the self descipline, your imagination can fly, turn dreams and nightmares into the stuff of fiction.

Science fiction by:

Isaac Asimov  
Arthur C. Clarke  
Harlan Ellison  
Ursula K. Le Guin  
Ray Bradbury  
Theodore Sturgeon  
Robert Silverberg  
J. R. R. Tolkien  

Cordwainer Smith  
Olaf Stapledon  
Robert Heinlein  
Jules Verne  
H. G. Wells  
John Brunner  
John W. Campbell, Jr.

# VI
## THE NOVELLA

STORY, AS THE MAGAZINE of the short story, also championed this longer form of fiction, and although practically no one else was printing them, novellas were featured among its pages. After *STORY* had launched the word, Edward J. O'Brien, editor of *The Best American Short Stories,* called attention to this revival of "a neglected form," the novella, in which Henry James, Thomas Mann, Ivan Bunin, and many others had done some of their finest work; and *STORY*'s continued publication of the novella gave currency and acceptance to the term as we use it here. "There is no word in English for the form," wrote Mr. O'Brien. "A novelette is a skeleton novel. A novella, on the contrary, is a story of sustained breath which accepts all the limitations of the short story unities." The word itself is Italian and means the same thing in that language as it does transplanted into English with its italics dropped; it parallels the *Novelle* in German and *nouvelle* in French.

The novella has been a fascinating attraction. The short story, however varied and unpredictable in the hands of its thousands of practitioners, has the uniformity of relative shortness; like the violin, its size has reached a norm. The novella, running anywhere from ten thousand to fifty thousand words in length, is like the viola. The viola, in a range of tone between the lyric fiddle and the full-bodied cello, has never yet been standardized, and no two violas have been found alike in length or breadth or in the depths they sound from their more than fiddle-sized bellies. The length and treatment in a novella grow out of the material and thought of its author. In the good, full shape of this fictional form, each author has time to develop what he has to say and to present it with full dramatic spaciousness—the frame is big enough. And it is a key to the honesty and artistry of the author that he has not tried to pad his tale into the length of a conventional novel.

"Once upon a time when I was a publisher," wrote the late Hirschel Brickel, "an author and I together ruined a fine piece of fiction which was exactly the length it needed to be by trying to stretch it into a novel of three hundred pages. This sad experience has often come back to me as I have watched with real satisfaction one after another of the arbitrary rules about how many words ought to go into a story, discarded and forgotten."

Actually, it would seem that O'Brien erred in one particular: the novella does not have to accept *all* "the limitations of the short story unities." While the technique *is* concentrated on achieving a single powerful effect, this may be achieved by more diverse methods.

To go back to "The Darling," by Chekhov, a story with which by now we are all familiar, the author did not permit himself to stray from his concentration on the one end of his story: the irony implicit in the lady's incapacity to change, no matter what the circumstances.

In the novella there may be a shifting in emphasis when other values, other threads of human consciousness and behavior occur tangential to the main theme. And the theme itself may seem to be one thing in the beginning, and then change as the tapeworm of the story moves it in another direction.

In Katherine Anne Porter's "Noon Wine" (first published in *STORY*), we meet Mr. Helton, a "tall bony man with straw-colored hair," as he arrives at the Thompson dairy. Mr. Thompson is described as "a noisy proud man who held his neck so straight his whole face stood level with his Adam's apple, and the whiskers continued down his neck and disappeared into a black thatch under his open collar." This description would seem to be only a plant to provide background for Mr. Helton, whom Mr. Thompson hires for a dollar a day.

Mr. Helton tells nothing about himself, except that he is Swedish from North Dakota, but he does his work better than it has been done before and the farm prospers. He plays the harmonica, and once when Mrs. Thompson goes to his room to compliment him on his work she sees a number of shiny harmonicas, "all good and expensive, standing in a row on the shelf beside his cot."

One day the two Thompson boys sneak into his room, and Mr. Helton catches them with his harmonicas. There is a suggestion of violence here, but Mrs. Thompson blames the boys and their father punishes them.

The years go on, Mr. Helton revealing no more about himself

than on the day he came, never talking, just playing his harmonicas, a "changeless tune went on, a strange tune, with sudden turns in it, night after night, and sometimes even in the afternoons when Mr. Helton sat down to catch his breath."

The Thompsons liked the music at first, but eventually they become tired of it. Yet it was the hired man's only pleasure, since he refused any other, even churchgoing when Mrs. Thompson invited him to go with them. He was also a calm man, except when the boys had gotten into his harmonicas, but this happened only once, and all goes well.

Until one day a fat stranger comes to the farm looking for "Mr. Olaf Eric Helton, from North Dakota." Around the corner of the house came the tune from Helton's harmonica.

Mr. Hatch, the visitor, says Mr. Helton used to play that tune in North Dakota, sitting "up in a straitjacket, practically, when he was in the asylum—"

Then it all comes out. Mr. Helton, it seems, had a brother who borrowed his harmonica one night to court his girl and lost it. And Mr. Helton "just ups, as I says, and runs his pitchfork through his brother"; he was committed to an asylum but escaped, and Mr. Hatch has come to take Helton back. He makes, he confesses, a tidy little sum from rounding up "escaped loonatics," and he's brought handcuffs with him. He expects Mr. Thompson will want to help him.

But Mr. Thompson suddenly becomes angry and protests that there is nothing wrong with the hired man now. "You're the crazy one around here, you're crazier than he ever was!" he shouts. And he orders Hatch off the place.

Mr. Helton comes around the corner with his arms swinging, his eyes wild, to step between the visitor and Mr. Thompson. The fat man dives at him with a knife.

"Mr. Thompson saw it coming, he saw the blade going in Mr. Helton's stomach, he knew he had the ax out of the log in his own hands, felt his arms go up over his head and bring the ax down on Mr. Hatch's head as if he were stunning a beef." And Mr. Helton then takes off into the woods.

If this had been written as a short story it probably would have ended here with some ironic closing last lines or ending to the situation. Perhaps Mr. Thompson would find that Mr. Helton is dangerous after all, and Mr. Hatch had simply wanted to save him.

Or that the fat man is a complete impostor so he, Thompson, had been right to mistrust him. A short story would not go on into another long development of the story, particularly concerning Mr. and Mrs. Thompson, once the problem with Mr. Helton has been solved. A conclusion would be found and a meaning based only on the story to this point.

Yet in the novella we go on another third of the way, with Mr. Thompson, who was after all acquitted of the murder, now insisting on driving about the countryside with Mrs. Thompson, day after day, stopping at all the neighboring houses and explaining over and over again how the thing had happened. Mrs. Thompson must back him up, crying most of the time, not because of Mr. Helton's death, but because this development is causing her to break down.

When her collapse comes, their two sons turn against their father, as have their friends and neighbors. They stand beside their mother's bed and stare as though their father were "a dangerous wild beast." The dissolution of the family is complete.

Mr. Thompson, with no fight left in him, tells the boys to look after their mother and goes out through the kitchen, where he takes a shotgun from the cupboard.

He writes a note, telling the story over again, saying he didn't take Hatch's life on purpose but only in defense of Mr. Helton. He then lies down flat, drawing the barrel of the gun under his chin so that he can pull the trigger with his big toe.

If Miss Porter had decided to write a novel, the proportions again would not have been the same. Each development would have been a chapter, each character would have been developed independently, on or off the scene. For example, we would be with the boys when they creep into Mr. Helton's cabin and take his harmonicas. We would feel their sense of mischief and also their apprehension, and we ourselves would feel suspense as the author shows him coming back toward his cabin, coming in unexpectedly and catching the boys, shaking them in his rage. We would be in on the degree of his anger, so that when Mr. Hatch finally reveals Mr. Helton's secret, we would have been prepared fully for it.

There would be a chapter in North Dakota early in the novel, showing the odious Mr. Hatch coming to see Helton's mother and then preparing for the trip. The mother is brought in distantly in the novella, for it is she who has given Mr. Hatch her son's address and the money to see her son. We would see Hatch as the threat he is, coming closer and closer to Mr. Helton, who has settled so solidly with the Thompsons.

There is already a novelistic quality to the ending, as in many novellas, perhaps a more visible logic than in a short story. But the ending could have been expanded to several chapters, showing the scenes most completely as Mr. Thompson makes his explanations. Time would not be jumped over; indeed, the trial itself would no doubt be a high point in a novel. And in the end, we would not just be told how the boys react to their father, since we have been with them in earlier scenes, we would also share their feelings, their shame, and their hatred. And Mr. Thompson's tragedy.

This third form of fiction is a particularly satisfying one to write; every writer should try at least one during his career, even though the market is almost nonexistent for the length. A novella has a place in a book, either as one of three or four, or with a collection of short stories, where it is generally the high point of the presentation.

We all recall the famous novellas of our century: *The Gentleman from San Francisco,* by Ivan Bunin; *Death in Venice,* by Thomas Mann; *The Turn of the Screw,* by Henry James; *Ethan Frome,* by Edith Wharton; *A Lost Lady,* by Willa Cather—and so many others, by Colette, by Alberto Moravia, by Isak Dinesen, Kay Boyle, D. H. Lawrence. Nearly all good writers have found themselves in this form, and our literature is the richer for their discoveries.

# VII
## ON BECOMING
## A PROFESSIONAL WRITER

THERE CAN BE FEW moments in life that extend one's horizons so happily as first acceptance of a short story or a novel. As in new love, or the birth of a baby, all roads seem open and brightly lighted to the skies; we have only to anticipate new discoveries, guard well our possessions, and prepare our packs for the excitement of the trek to follow.

No one has written more eloquently of the beginnings of success than F. Scott Fitzgerald: "And then, suddenly, everything changed, and this article is about that first wild wind of success and the delicious mist it brings with it. It is a short and precious time.

". . . The postman rang, and that day I quit work and ran along the streets, stopping automobiles to tell friends and acquaintances about it—my novel *This Side of Paradise* was accepted for publication. That week the postman rang and rang, and I paid off my terribly small debts, bought a suit, and woke up every morning with a world of ineffable top-loftiness and promise.

"While I waited for the novel to appear, the metamorphosis of amateur into professional began to take place—a sort of stitching together of your whole life into a pattern of work, so that the end of one job is automatically the beginning of another. I had been an amateur before; in October, when I strolled with a girl among the stones of a southern graveyard, I was a professional."

In a letter Thomas Wolfe wrote to Sherwood Anderson, he said: "I think I am starving for publication: I love to get published; it maddens me not to get published. I feel at times like getting every publisher in the world by the scruff of his neck, forcing his jaws open, and cramming the Mss. down his throat—'God-damn you, here it is—I will and must be published.'

"You know what it means—you're a writer and you understand

it. It's not just 'the satisfaction of being published.' Great God! It's the satisfaction of getting it *out,* or having that, so far as you're concerned, gone through with it! That good or ill, for better or for worse, it's over, done with, finished, out of your life forever and that, come what may, you can at least, as far as this thing is concerned, get the merciful damned easement of oblivion and forgetfulness.''

Writers tend to be jumpy, nervous creatures between books. They like to get on with something else, and too often old doubts set in. Few writers have the persistence of scientists, who check, recheck, and wait for developments, although there was persistence if not patience in Thomas Wolfe. John Napier, the Scottish discoverer of logarithms, worked on figures endlessly until it "worked out"—in fourteen years. A novel may take a year, or two years, or five. And the times between may take as long.

The writer's position is somewhat different from anybody else's. Most of his material—perhaps all, as in the case of Wolfe—has been his own life. The material is there. The writing is the laboratory in which he tests it for results.

Some years after his first successes as a writer, William Saroyan wrote for *STORY* on being a writer, an article called "Art and Imbecility": "First, it was preposterous—it was for me, at any rate —for anybody to declare point blank that he is a writer. The effect of this declaration on society—well, they don't like it. It's not a nice declaration to make. Society wants to know who you think you are to be a writer, and there is no ready answer to that. The writer is driven underground and goes about his business with all the secrecy of the anarchist-revolutionist he very likely is anyway. . . .

"But it soon came to pass that I—carrying on as I was—came to be published, and soon after came to be famous, too. I think I may say in all truth and innocence that while I was stunned enough to be published at last at the age of twenty-five, I did not find fame anything at all like a *new* circumstance, for I had for quite a long time felt as famous as any man ought to feel who does not intend eventually to go berserk with the foolishness and wreak some terrible mischief on unsuspecting multitudes. I mean I had felt for a long time famous enough for all practical purposes, and to this day I have never found it odd that even established middle-classers have never heard of me or read anything I have ever written.''

The time it takes to arrive at being a professional writer is seldom predictable. Chances are that sometime before the world recognizes us, other things have been taking place in our minds, our controls, and our self-image. Saroyan had "felt for a long time famous enough for all practical purposes"; readiness is an important stage too often ignored in such chronicles. By this time the writer has hurdled the disbelief in his own work and talent *in his own mind,* and has become indifferent to the skepticism of others; he has become increasingly adept at self-criticism and is ready and humble enough to listen to the criticism of an editor, to take his advice and aid seriously enough to learn even more than he thinks he knows already.

Writing to him is no longer a matter of primarily secret pleasures (although this feeling may never be entirely absent in the dedicated writer, or lover); he knows writing is also a job, and when a contract is at stake he knows it is a moral obligation to produce the work he has promised after a payment of money in exchange.

To be a professional writer and not an amateur, one must arrange to spend at least two-thirds of his working and/or thinking time on his writing. To convince an editor or publisher that he is ready for a contract, a professional writer should be able to show previously published work and provide an original outline for the projected task acceptable to the publisher; or he must offer a piece of work in itself so nearly complete and perfect that the editor realizes only minor revisions will be required.

In the case of a short story, seldom will an editor suggests changes and improvements *before* buying a story. He may suggest these afterwards, and sometimes you will take them and sometimes you will not. Sometimes it is better if you do not. Certain very large circulation magazines will have reasons other than literary ones to suggest changes: it may be that they want a happy ending where a more equivocal ending has been more honest; an English magazine will want to place your story in the English countryside instead of in Montana, say, for their own "reader identification."

In the matter of the first suggestion, you will have to consult your conscience, but beware. That story will exist forever in your dossier, long after the few thousands (or hundreds) of dollars have been spent.

In the matter of the second, geographical changes or others of equal value, perhaps it does not matter.

At *STORY,* we generally found that a story was acceptable as it was, or that it didn't interest us. Not all editors have the freedom of choice we had, which of course permitted us to recognize and delight in the unique talent of an author, answering to no other judgment than our own standards of excellence. Our reputation was secure: Whit's genius through forty years of editing made this so.

What did we look for in the unsolicited manuscripts of an unknown author?

First, as with all readers for all publications, we wanted an arresting, or provocative, or mood-invoking, or character-interesting first paragraph. We have said this before, but it cannot be stressed too much, particularly in the writing of a short story.

We wanted a logical and interesting carryover into the next paragraph, and the next and the next—in other words, we expected our attention to be held straight through to the end with no effort on our part. It was as simple as that!

Besides this, we insisted that the author have authority, in knowledge of his material, his psychology, and his background. That he make us *believe,* and believe that he also *believed.* It is unlikely that a young Puerto Rican writer from Brooklyn could write convincingly of the backwoods of William Faulkner, or that a male misogynist would arouse our emotions over the abortion dilemma of an adolescent girl.

We rejected sentimentality; self-conscious metaphors; narcissistic writing in which the author obviously sees herself as irresistible; pornography for the sake of pornography—although an editor of *Playboy* once told Whit that it would be hard for them to "get away" with some of our stories, because ours were first of all considered "literature."

We were probably guilty of impatience with a badly typed and misspelled, soiled manuscript; and agents who sent in stories by the dozens which obviously had been rejected by every other magazine in the world seldom proved to have anything of value for us. But we read them: God knows we read them all!

Perhaps the best advice for the short story writer would be not to aim too high professionally at the start. The best "young" work is, as everyone knows, generally seen first in the small magazines, and it is read by the editors of the two major collections, *The Best American Short Stories* and the O. Henry collections. Yet certain conscientious editors of the large circulation magazines very often are interested in the new, unknown writer and may offer helpful advice or encouragement.

Alice Morris, when she was editor of *Harper's Bazaar,* wrote a revealing letter to the author of this book: "The story that goes fastest into the rejection pile here is the one that shows lack of literary perception and skill. Many young writers, I feel, have stories to tell but don't bother to perfect the tools by which to tell them. Sentences are awkward, dialogue either totally banal or totally unconvincing (unlifelike)—thus, no matter how interesting or valid the theme, it comes to nothing in the end. Obviously, a skilled writer can take practically any theme and turn it into gold—he infuses it with the magic of art, and manages to *illuminate some particular angle of living.*

"Also, or perhaps it is even paramount, the writer must learn to dramatize his theme, rather than delivering it by exposition. Too many stories are *told,* rather than *happening.* On this depends, too, the success of the story at capturing the reader. No matter how sensitive, perceptive, etc., a writer may be, if he doesn't manage to get a grip on the reader by page 2, he's done for.

"The quality I look for in the stories that pass over my desk is primarily, I suppose, a combination of vitality, freshness and illumination. Don't know how else to put it!"

It is unlikely any other editor looking for short stories could put it better.

As for the novel, most of what applies to the short story may be said of the novel as well, plus, of course, the ability to carry on "vitality, freshness and illumination" for three or four hundred pages. Both techniques are difficult and demanding. Each form must be understood and mastered in its own particularity.

I have asked Joe Vergara, my editor at Harper & Row, to describe how publishers view fiction from their side of the editorial desk. Here are his comments:

"How do editors choose the fiction they publish? When they read manuscripts, what are they looking for? Hardly a cocktail party goes by that an editor isn't asked these or similar questions. Too often, I'm afraid, the questioner is disappointed with what seems a vague or evasive answer. The truth is that editors tend to develop their own general guidelines, but there are no infallible rules, no trustworthy checklists to guide them. (And luckily for editors, for who would need them otherwise?)

"In assessing nonfiction, the editor is on firmer ground. Is the subject of interest to a specific audience? Are there competing books? Does the author have attention-getting credentials? Has the author uncovered new dramatic facts? Can he present his material in an organized, interesting way? Does his book make a contribution in its field?

"These are straightforward questions susceptible of straightforward answers. A bit of research, a study of competing books, a chat with the salesmen, and the editor is pointed toward a decision.

"Working with fiction isn't so straightforward. The editor (or anybody) can usually spot the hopeless manuscripts and just as often the highly professional efforts. How to judge all those in between? The editor can look for honesty, style, suspense, revealing insights. Will the reader care about the characters and what happens to them? Is the background colorful and convincing? If the author uses action, sex, and violence, do they flow naturally from the story and contribute to it, or are they dragged in every ten pages to pep things up? Does the work as a whole make an impact? Having considered these elements, and more, the editor must then fall back on his or her emotional reactions to the manuscript, taste, judgment, and an occasional dash of intuition."

Joan Kahn, Harper's editor of suspense novels (and an author herself), has this to say about selecting manuscripts to publish:

"There are books I like, and those are the books I have published. They have interested *me*—so I hope they will interest someone else. And they are well enough written so that the author's handling of the English language (that splendid means of conveying what's in his mind) serves his purpose, in which case his reader will be well served."

Ann Harris, Harper editor of *The Exorcist* and much other fiction and nonfiction puts it this way:

"A novel has got to immerse the reader in what is going on—the events of the plot, the innards of the characters—so that he or she wants to stay with it to the end.

"This is the primary criterion for whether it seems publishable. It applies whether the book is a work of literary quality or commercial potential or both, whether it uses experimental techniques or follows so classically simple a form as the pure detective story. To care about what is happening and watch it build, to *involve* the reader—this is the essential accomplishment."

Perhaps it adds up to this: no one can guarantee success to the writer of fiction. But publishers must publish, as authors must write. So write what excites you, write about characters that intrigue you,

write about events that move you. Criticize your work. Be merciless
with your efforts. And then write some more.

The professional knows, or thinks he knows, why he does what
he does, that is, writes. Robert Graves, both poet and prose writer,
thinks writers may be divided into categories to include those who
write for (1) money, (2) fame, (3) fun, (4) escape, (5) dire need,
and (6) miscellaneous reasons. He believes 55 percent of prose
writers fall into group 1; that is, money is the dominant reason they
write. Eighteen percent write for fame, 15 percent for fun, 7 percent
for escape, 4 percent out of dire need, and 1 percent for miscellaneous reasons.

Now Mr. Graves's six observations may be all very sound and may
explain why writers write; but each story or novel is a separate act
of writing, and probably no two had the same conception or reason
for existence.

If the professional is one who can do the same thing twice, accept-
ably, he has learned to know where, how, and in what he performs
best. He will not, however, stop there, with endless repetitions of
his first success. His growth as an artist involves enlargement of his
repertoire, adding technique to technique, and renewed promises to
his audience of continuing growth and increasing stature.

The professional knows there is more than one way to do things,
and many ways that sometimes mix. He may write for money and
still do a work of stature; he may write for fun and be serious
underneath. He may write to reveal the truth in his soul, and it may
still be the truth for others. He may set out to teach and end in
learning. He may amuse and at the same time instruct.

It all depends on what he means his fiction to be and to reflect.
His total view? His partial view? The views and philosophy of his
characters? The times he writes about? The tragedy of man? The
comedy of man? Or could it be just a simple, natural "story" as it
seems to him, and the people in it, serving no other end than to show
how people looked and thought and acted when some crisis in their
lives made a "story" of their actions?

"Yet the aspiring, no less than the humble, must grapple with
economic problems when writing fiction," wrote Bernard DeVoto.
He goes on to point out that it takes six months to ten years to write
a novel, "and neither the Guggenheim Foundation nor admiring
relatives will continue their subsidies forever."

Sherwood Anderson wrote in *STORY:* "A good many do it for money. It seems such an easy way. It isn't so easy. I have never yet known one of our commercial writers who was very happy. There are too many concessions to be made."

Yet Norman Mailer is reportedly not unhappy about his contract with his publisher arranging to pay him one million dollars for the rights to his next novel. Nor have the pressures seemed in any way to detract from the integrity of his work.

A further success story may be inserted here: Horatio Alger, Jr., according to his biographer, Ralph D. Gardner, has sold an estimated 400,000,000 copies of his books about boys-on-the-way-to-the-top, in thousands of editions, and is again on the upswing. Most writers, however, must settle for less.

But let us say the writer has sold his first novel or his story, and now feels he is on his way. The second novel, he has heard, is notoriously harder: harder to place, to please with, and even to write. But he does not believe this is true for him. Already he is started on a new project, perhaps on new ground this time; certainly no writer wants simply to repeat his first success.

Unfortunately there is almost no writer alive who can sit down and bat out one story or book after another, all of equal value. Every writer has his ups and downs, and it is usually immediately following his first success that he discovers them. A short story writer may write one perfect story and then three or four bad ones, or stories that do not sell. A novelist may have caught the fancy of reviewers first time out and then find his second novel ignored; or his second work may not please as much as the first, and this is uncomfortably and cruelly pointed out to him.

Fitzgerald, toward the end of his career, when he wrote "The Crackup" (three articles for *Esquire* magazine), spoke of the writer's inability to always produce work of which he could be proud. And yet: "I never blame failure—there are too many complicated situations in life—but I am absolutely merciless toward lack of effort."

Some writers stop at this point and write no more, having discovered that writing is not all fun; stories do not always come out of thin air and chirp in the author's ear, begging to be set down in his own inimitable style. The feeling of life that makes a novel may simply not spring from the subject matter as before.

"To continue to write is as trying as to begin," said Elizabeth Bowen. "Every step forward brings us into an area of new dangers, involving a summoning of powers which may not be there." Even after one has acquired a "name," she adds, "a name is not simply donated; it must be earned, and maintained."

Dylan Thomas said, "Any possible success is bad for me. . . . I should be what I was . . . twenty years ago. Then I was arrogant and lost. Now I am humble and found, I prefer that other."

The judgment of his peers perhaps means more to the author than other praise, with the exception of his own evaluation of himself.

William Faulkner told Harvey Breit in 1956 that he'd been asked to name the best writers in the country, and that he'd put "Wolfe first, myself second, then Hemingway, and Dos Passos and Caldwell last." But he went on to say, "I said we were all failures. All of us had failed to match the dream of perfection and I rated the authors on the basis of their splendid failure to do the impossible."

Wolfe came first, because "he tried to reduce all human existence to literature." Then, after Wolfe, "I tried the most." But Hemingway "just stayed within what he knew. He did it fine, but didn't try for the impossible."

Faulkner concluded unhappily: "The work never matches the dream of perfection the artist has to start with."

In various anthologies, notably *This Is My Best* and *The World's Best*, Whit asked the authors: "What do you consider your best work?" And sometimes he asked why a story was written. What was the genesis of the story, or book? How had they become writers in the first place? What were their greatest influences? What can they tell about writing as they themselves have experienced the labor?

Whit found in the first *This Is My Best*, for example, that "when someone dislikes a poem of Robert Frost's it takes the poet a long time to regain his original affection for it; that Mr. Hemingway has been represented so many times for some of his things that now he can hardly bear to look at what every high-school student, through the usual anthologies, thinks is his only mood. It was interesting to learn that neither the publishers nor the author thinks the much anthologized 'Paul's Case' by Willa Cather is either her best or her most representative work; and one was to learn that some authors cannot read their old works, or that when they do, they do so with the utmost pain and difficulty, and that still some others think the work they did twenty years ago is as good or better than their present writing."

Conrad Aiken, who selected the short story "Strange Moonlight" as his favorite work, explained it this way: "This little story is largely autobiographical, as will be obvious to anyone, and that may be one reason why the author has always been fond of it. But there is another reason as well. For I think when a writer makes over or partly makes over, his experience into a poem or story, he will then tend to forget the experience itself . . . it's as if he had put it into cold storage. Thereafter, when he wants to revisit that particular glimpse of the moon, he will find it more accessible, and far vivider, in the artifact than in his own recollection."

Norman Mailer considered *An American Dream* his best book, judging it as Faulkner judged his peers, because "I tried far more in this novel than anywhere else, and hence was living for a while with themes not easily accessible to literary criticism, not even to examination."

John Hersey wrote cheerfully: "I imagine, like any other writer, that my best work is yet to come—probably tomorrow morning I shall write it. Yes, tomorrow morning. Wait and see! For now, I have chosen these pages from *A Single Pebble*."

Bernard Malamud liked his story "The Jewbird," which was "inspired by Howard Nemerov's 'Digressions Around a Crow' . . . about a talking bird, and I said to myself, thinking of a jewfish, suppose the bird had been Jewish. At that point the story came to life."

Jesse Stuart preferred his story "Love in the Spring," because it came out of his world, the hill and mountain country of eastern Kentucky. "If it is durable enough to last," he wrote, "it is because my world is real."

Joseph Heller liked the historical implications of a scene with "Lieutenant Scheisskopf, because it is most fully descriptive of the native dangers we faced in those days and contains my sharpest mockery of the people responsible for them."

Philip Roth's favorite passage is from *Portnoy's Complaint*—"a novel in the form of a monologue by a psychoanalytic patient—for the way it *moves:* the way it announces its subject—'Oh, this father!' —and then proceeds to explore the ambiguities of feeling and the recollected experiences that call forth these three opening words and their exclamation point."

Perhaps there is only one way to conclude this book, and that is to describe an old cartoon from *The New Yorker* magazine that Whit kept over his desk, which may show better than any other example the difference between the professional and the amateur.

Two pottery-making Indians in Mexico are sitting in the sun before two puzzled-looking American tourists. One peddler is surrounded by his work—jugs, vases, dishes, and pots of all shapes and sizes. The other fellow sits half asleep in front of his single pot. Evidently the tourists have asked him if this one pot is all he has. The caption under the cartoon reads: "Why make more? I haven't sold this one yet."

The professional writer keeps on writing, and even if it takes a very long time to sell his pots, he doesn't stop making them. For it is the act of writing, the goal of perfecting our talents, the pleasures of using new experiences and older memories, new loves and old sentiments, of keeping alive the senses and sharpening the wits, finding ever-deeper meanings and colors in the clay itself, that absorbs us to the end.

The writer will of course expect to be published. He will pray to all the gods he knows for a sympathetic and intelligent editor, and on publication, for understanding critics and enthusiastic readers; and he will know that his part in all this is simple. He has only to deliver the goods.

Henry Miller wrote at the age of sixty-five, after a lifetime's defiance and many books of apparently unalterable self-admiration: "Even now I do not consider myself a writer, in the ordinary sense of the word. I am a man telling the story of his life, a process which appears more and more inexhaustible. Like the world evolution, it is endless. It is a turning inside out and voyaging through $X$ dimension, with the result that somewhere along the way one discovers that what one has to tell is not nearly so important as the telling itself."

# A SALUTE TO WHIT BURNETT
# 1899–1972

## by J. D. Salinger

BACK IN 1939, when I was twenty, I was a student for a time in one of the present editors'—Whit Burnett's—short-story course, up at Columbia. A good and instructive and profitable year for me, on all counts, let me briefly say. Mr. Burnett simply and very knowledgeably conducted a short-story course, never mugwumped over one. Whatever personal reasons he may have had for being there, at all, he plainly had no intentions of using fiction, short or long, as a leg up for himself in the academic or quarterly-magazine hierarchies. He usually showed up for class late, praises on him, and contrived to slip out early—I often have my doubts whether any good and conscientious short-story-course conductor can humanly do more. Except that Mr. Burnett did. I have several notions how or why he did, but it seems essential only to say that he had a passion for good short fiction, strong short fiction, that very easily and properly dominated the room. It was clear to us that he loved getting his hands on *any* body's excellent story—Bunin's or Saroyan's, Maupassant's or Dean Fales' or Tess Slessinger's, Hemingway's or Dorothy Parker's or Clarence Day's, and so on, no particular pets, no fashionable prejudices. He was there, unmistakably, and however reechy it is almost sure to sound, in the service of the Short Story. But I would not ask Mr. Burnett to bear with any further hoarse praise from me. Not quite, anyway, of the same ilk.

Here is something that has stuck in my mind for over twenty-five years.

In class, one evening, Mr. Burnett felt himself in the mood to read Faulkner's "That Evening Sun Go Down" out loud, and he went right ahead and did it. A rapid reading, among other things, most singularly and undescribably low-key. In effect, he was much less reading the story aloud than running through it, verbatim, and very thoughtfully, with about twenty-five percent of his voice open. Almost anybody picked at random from a crowded subway car would have given a more dramatic or "better" performance. But that was just the point. Mr. Burnett very deliberately forbore to perform. He abstained from reading beautifully. It was as if he had turned himself into a reading lamp, and his voice into paper and print. By and large, he left you on your own to know how the characters were saying what they were saying. You got your Faulkner story straight, without any middlemen between. Not before or since have I heard a reader make such instinctive and wholehearted concessions to a born printed-page writer's needs and, aye, rights. Regretfully, I never got to meet Faulkner, but I often had it in my head to shoot him a letter telling him about that unique reading of Mr. Burnett's. In this nutty, exploitive era, people who read short stories beautifully are all over the place—recording, taping, podiumizing, televising—and I wanted to tell Faulkner, who must have heard countless moving interpretations of his work, that not once, throughout the reading, did Burnett come between the author and his beloved silent reader. Whether he has ever done it again, I don't know, but with somebody who has brought the thing off even once, the written short-story form must be very much at home, intact, unfinagled with, suitably content.

Salutes to Whit Burnett, to Hallie Burnett, and to all *STORY* readers and contributors.

J.D.S.

(*From a previously unpublished preface to a book by Hallie and Whit Burnett.*)

# INDEX